Every Leader Needs Followers:

10 Keys to Transform Restaurant Managers to Hospitality Leaders

Never Lead Alone Again

Jason E. Brooks

HospiVation, LLC

York, SC

Published by, HospiVation, LLC
214 Harrowfield Hts., York SC 29745
http://www.jasonebrooks.com

The information presented herein represents the view of the author as of the date of publication. This nook is presented for informational purposes only. Due to the rate at which conditions change, the author reserves the right to alter and update his opinions based on new conditions. While every attempt has been made to verify the information in this book, neither the author nor his affiliates/partners assume any responsibility for errors, inaccuracies, or omissions.

Cover design by Yasir Nadeem
Interior design by Dan Notra
Printed in the USA

Every Leader Needs Followers: 10 Keys to Transform Restaurant Managers to Hospitality Leaders / Jason E. Brooks. -- 1st ed.
ISBN   979-8-9898091-2-7

To Ronda, Jenna, Nassir, & Aiden. You are my family and my best friends.

Thank you to the industry professionals who took the time to answer interview questions for quotes among the various topics in this book. Kimberly Grant, Pat Peterson, Alan McGee, David Baldasaro, Sean Keyes, Paul Macaluso, Mike Moore, Steve Taylor, Coley O'Brien, Ranita Bullock, Julie Thompson, Gerald Pulsinelli. You all have ever-changing, hectic schedules that leave little time for a few things, and you made time to make this a part of it. I can't thank you enough.

To my mother Jeanette Boler, and my father John Brooks, Sr. Thank you for raising me to have the right balance of love, hospitality, compassion, and professionalism. I can only hope to continue making you proud parents and follow your lead in life.

Contents

Introduction

What's the one thing every person needs to be a leader?

Followers.

There's no two ways around it. No fancy multi-hyphenated titles, flashy business cards, or name drops can shortcut the fact that no matter how much you stand in the middle of a meeting thumping your chest screaming, you'll never be a leader without followers, period.

Ask any socialite: even after getting people to follow you, you still must work hard at keeping them.

I don't think we realize the power of following today. Nearly every form of media we interact with, whether a song, movie, streaming service, or LinkedIn – it is all via the power of follower generation. Half the time, we don't realize we are doing it, and if we do, we don't even know why. We just click the button because that's how we recognize something that intrigues us or that we aspire to be like.

We follow. And there's nothing wrong with that.

Let's take the example of your cell phone. It's just a tool. Everyone around you has one. On the contrary, does everyone around you have a million followers? No, but some people do. There are influencers that have created a pattern of time management that makes gaining a million followers look easy, they have turned this into their tool. Not only have influencers created a pattern of management to gain followers, but they have also created a pattern of management for keeping them. Although, the tool is only as good as the person that wields it. This book is designed to help you create those followers and keep them.

I know this is beginning to sound like a manual about social media, but this is one of the core understandings you must have to be a restaurant leader or any leader in an organization, for that matter. This is also one of the main reasons leaders get frustrated or fail in their positions. They do not realize leadership is a two-way road involving people and their desire to follow you. Those who choose not to comprehend this just end up as another manager in a blue polo on a trek by themselves.

This book will give you the ten best keys to transform from a Restaurant Manager to a Hospitality Leader and build success in your building while doing so. Not just build success but build an organized team around you to get you to a state where you will never lead alone again. It does this by giving you repeatable steps that increase whole team ownership within your organization, from tenured employees to new hires.

It starts with simple things that get overlooked in your day-to-day whirlwind that are in fact priceless gems that make you and your team shine in the guest's eyes and the eyes of your peers.

This book isn't written in chronological order, so you can skip to different chapters as needed. However, I implore that you read all sections at some point to help perfect your leadership style.

Each chapter will focus on one of ten keys in leadership that help connect you with the pulse of your restaurant/bakery/bar/shop. In between some of the chapters are side notes that are slight diversions of the ten keys to your transformation, but are important foundational steps to keep in mind. Each key has three sections.

The Main Course – the largest, most important part of your mental meal.

The Takeaway – a quick one to two-minute overview of the main course for those who have less time on their hands or need a quick reminder of the chapter.

The Angle – a gallery of quotes from some of the most impressive and influential people I've had the honor to work or connect with.

How did I end up with ten keys, you ask? Great question! First, it's a pretty solid number to remember. Second, we could easily think of 100 steps, but these ten work in multiple situations throughout your week to help make your role easier. Third, who doesn't want to write a 'Ten Best' book?

But what makes me an expert on restaurant leadership? Another great question!

No, I did not open a restaurant in Maine and receive three James Beard awards.

I am not the executive chef of a 3 Michelin Star establishment.

I haven't partnered with celebrities to own multiple eateries across the globe.

I wasn't even a contestant on Chopped.

I simply know my numbers, know my people, and make my team better when they leave me from when I first hired them.

Every. Single. One.

Even after they do leave (voluntarily & involuntarily), my prior team still reaches out for tips to help build their leadership skills.

I've used all of these lessons and skills I've learned over 30+ years to now help executives through coaching, through workshops, and motivate crowds of 1000s as a keynote speaker.

Transforming from a manager to a leader is one success story but having that equate to opportunities that net financial gain because of your new reputation is icing on the cake. That's where I want you to be. Eating icing off the cake and teaching your team to do the same.

See, I'm what some would call a restaurant lifer.

I started banging out dishes at the age of 15 in a mom-and-pop seafood restaurant in Fayetteville, NC. Graduating to pantry, making salads and desserts a year later, onto prep, then the flat top grill, then char grill, then sauté. I was on FIRE! I've been a Sous Chef, Kitchen Manager, Bar Manager, Service Manager, GM, Managing Partner, Director of Operations, Franchise Business Consultant, and Franchise Operations Coach.

At a young age, I learned how to hustle by nature, and I had a pretty good head on my shoulders. The sky was the limit for most, but I knew I was bound for more.

By day, I was an up-and-coming cook with a Wusthof knife kit.

At night I was making underground music with my friends. Being that I had the hustle gene in me, I didn't just stop at writing lyrics and recording music.

I wrote pitches to program directors, music directors, music columnists, and editors, getting our music into the hands of radio stations across the country and in music publications on the East and West Coast.

I could easily speak with club promoters to get us live gigs for a cut of the door. Connecting with a stranger and finding a middle ground to success was always easy.

That's what we do daily in hospitality.

Back then we created our own flyers, stickers, and album

covers. Mixed & mastered our own sounds, and we were the head of our own promotions.

We hustled.

But during my second year in college, I faced a hard reality. Either keep going to college and probably end up broke from not making ends meet, or drop out and work full time.

That's when I became one of the 45%s, according to Slate.com, that drop out of college in pursuit of something else.

Eventually, I saw that the same perseverance, determination, and structured mindset I put into music led me to a lot of open doors and opportunities in the hospitality industry.

By no means am I endorsing dropping out of school. Nor would I endorse putting your rent money on a dice roll from someone else's hand. It just ended up being my situation and a choice I made. That was my fate and mine alone.

Would I do it again to end up here right now? Hell yes.

Through it all, I've worked for over 20 different brands. I've seen the Mona Lisa painted 20 different ways. Some renditions of Mona were great, and some just plain pieces of work.

Seeing the vision and hearing the gospel of 50 different Presidents and CEOs gives one insight on many key pieces of leadership. But sometimes, it just boils down to what you won't do when you find yourself in a position to lead.

I've hired over 400 General Managers, Assistant Managers, and Shift Leaders.

Hired another 2500+ employees.

I've interviewed nearly 8000 candidates and personally screened over 25,000 resumes and applications.

I learned quickly that leadership isn't something that only happens in boardrooms and on quarterly earnings calls. It isn't something that's reviewed annually during performance meetings.

It's the culmination of the personalities in the people you put around you that can see the vision.

It's something that happens when you find that people who surround you not only look to you for the right answer but trust, believe, and follow the very words you utter. Because it is their words too.

If you find yourself or your team struggling to find the right direction, words, or energy to get your business back on track, reach out to me on www.jasonebrooks.com. Click Connect at the top of the page so we can talk through what you feel success should look like in our four walls, and I how I can help you get there. Please sign up for my email list as well to stay up to date on upcoming events in your area, as well as leadership tips to help you tackle your day, week, and life.

Lastly, everyone that purchases a book gets a copy of my Delegation Template and One-on-One Template. When you click on connect on the website, type 'Free Templates' in the more about section and I'll send you both templates referenced in this book for free.

Let's get right into it. The 10 Keys to Transform from a Restaurant Manager to a Hospitality Leader.

Master Your KPIs

The Main Course

KPI stands for Key Performance Indicator. As you most likely know, restaurant speak involves a lot of acronyms.

ULE - Unit Level Economics

AUV - Average Unit Volume

AOR - Area of Responsibility

BOH - Back of House

FOH - Front of House

CAPEX - Capital Expenditure

CBT - Computer Based Training

COGS - Cost of Goods Sold

EOD - End of Day

R&M - Repair & Maintenance

MIT - Manager in Training

LSM - Local Store Marketing

YTD - Year to Date

PTD - Period to Date

WTD - Week to Date

TTT - Train the Trainer

This list goes on and on. You name it, we have an acronym for it. If not, we'll make one tomorrow because saying it faster is better… said no one ever.

The key takeaway to this chapter is to master your KPIs (and what the acronyms mean) because this is how your brand and your direct supervisor will grade you.

Most managers believe it's as simple as knowing what sales were last year, and what the goal is this year. The same goes for traffic count, check average, add on sales, food cost, and labor. And if your owner is open enough to share this with you, EBITDA, or cash flow after everything is paid for. These are important, but let's look closer at what pushes your business to success and who controls that.

Fundamentally, you need to know three sets of KPIs. The first KPI is the one your entire brand sets its goals on annually that gets reported to the shareholders.

The second set is the one your direct supervisor reviews with you weekly, quarterly, and annually. This is the one you will be repeatedly graded on.

The last set is the one you know moves the mark in your location. Because every location is different, even if the restaurant has the same menu, logo, and uniforms. What success means in each location will vary widely.

Let's start with the first set of KPIs. We'll call it Brand Level KPIs. Brand Level is the overarching goal for the company to reach by the end of its fiscal year. These are the true Big Rock goals for the company. Knowing this is key to you being viewed as a key player that contributes to the brand's success.

The caveat to this is not every Brand goal makes sense in your location. You could be consistently surpassing 2 of the 3 Big Rock goals every period, making your priorities shift elsewhere. On the other hand, you can be so far off from meeting those goals that there are fundamentals you need to worry about first to improve the foundation to get anywhere close to these goals. But always knowing what those goals are and making the day-to-day effort to reach or exceed them needs to stay top of mind for you and your team.

Up next is your Direct Supervisor's KPIs. To get these, you must be very clear when coming on board to ask what KPIs that you will be held to for your reviews. If you're already in position as the manager, you need to review these with your direct supervisor each period as sometimes their focus will change. This set of KPIs is extremely important as this is what you will be held to by the person who will be giving your reviews.

You may have some room for negotiation here. For example, let's say your Brand Level's In-Store Comp Sales growth target for the year is 3%. They also want 5% in Catering, and 2% in Traffic growth. These Brand Level goals will usually roll straight down to your Direct Supervisor, then to you for your location.

If last year you were down -1.5% in in-store comp sales, and flat in traffic, plus down -0.5% in Catering, you would be hard-pressed to reach those goals. For you to hit them you would have to grow sales 3.5%, traffic 2%, and Catering 5.5%. I would suggest giving the more realistic goal that gives you the 3% comp sales increase over last year, versus making up the negative loss plus an additional 3% to get to the Brand Level KPI goal.

Or, your boss can just say 'Screw that, get me 3% positive

comps', and you go about your merry way to make it happen.

The point is to understand the gravity of what your Direct Supervisor wants you to accomplish, translate it to your restaurant's current performance and meet in the middle where it's a reachable goal while putting pressure on your team to execute and surpass that.

Lastly, is your store level KPIs. This is where you create and hone the foundations of your restaurant so it operates soundly, and where you can incorporate your assistant managers and shift leaders to make things happen.

Success in this is best done in small pieces to make it digestible for your team. For example, if your year-end goal is 5% in Catering growth, break your catering sales up by the month. For the first month, your goal for your team is to increase catering sales by 1%. If your total catering sales for last year are $6000 for the month, they need an additional $60 for each of the first month. That's most likely 1 additional catering order over last year. Sounds easy right?

If most sales gurus are correct, it takes 20 'Nos' to get to a 'Yes'. This means your catering manager needs to market to 5 additional businesses per week to drum up one additional catering order by the end of the 4-week period. For the second and third months, up the target goal to 2%. Month 4 & 5 to 3%, and so on until you can move your team with momentum to hit the 5% by year end in total catering sales.

Breaking down your KPIs to these three basic segments will help you to better manage your business, put it in actionable targets to make the Brand hit its targets, keep your Direct Supervisor happy, and help drive your team with digestible goals to bring success to light.

But now that you understand your three levels of KPIs, what do you do with them to help lead your team and keep them on track?

The answer is scoreboards.

No not the cheesy ones that have glitter all over the border (but if that works for you, no judgment from me!) I'm talking about Scoreboards that help teach the team what Lag and Lead measures are on big goals, and how your team contributes to making those happen shift to shift. Below is a great example of a location's Scoreboard to help build their Guest Service scores on their survey

Grow Goal in Guest Service to 85%

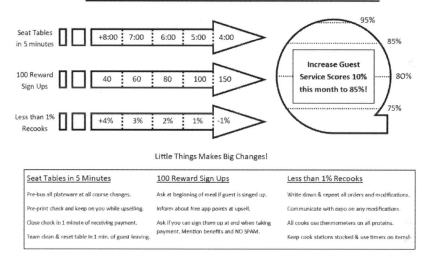

As you can see, their main goal is to grow Guest Service scores to 85%. This is the LAG measure. The point of success. They then have three LEAD measures to help support it and get them there by - seating all tables in 5 minutes of quoted wait, signing up 100 new guests to their rewards program, and having less than 1% recooks for every item that goes out the kitchen.

At the bottom of each scoreboard are different tips on what each employee can do to help reach those LEAD measures that support the LAG measure.

The three lead measures show the set goal as well as some Stretch Goals if they happen to surpass their initial goal line.

The next question is, who keeps up with the Scoreboards?

I always suggest using your key players in this. This can make it more competitive! For seating tables in 5 minutes, your head host can help keep up with the timers on each shift and update the dashboard at the end of each week. It's best to have a mini dashboard and timer on the clipboard at the host stand to keep up with the day-to-day stats.

Your service or marketing manager keeps up with the reward sign-ups. In this example, updates can be posted when it hits each interval of 20 sign-ups.

Lastly, your culinary or kitchen manager can update the Recook scoreboard, as well as ensure that stations are set for peak volume, bodies are in place, proper pacing of food items is being coordinated with the back expo, and checklists are completed daily.

To make your scoreboard interactive, have a big prize for reaching the main goal, as well as mini prizes for success along the way. Here are some examples of mini goals/prizes:

Server with the highest check average.

Person seen bussing the most tables other than theirs.

Cook with no recooks.

Cook with perfect temps.

Server with most Reward Program sign-ups.

Host with perfect wait time quotes.

These are just a few examples to help reinforce the habits that support the end result. Raising the Guest Service scores to 85% or higher.

Now, you have your KPIs from your brand, your KPIs from your Direct Supervisor, your store-level KPIs, a Dashboard to house the information, and prizes to help keep the competitive juices flowing. But where do you put it? Great question!

For some reason, anytime important information needs to be posted, it ends up near the back door by the employee rack only to be seen when one is clocking in and out. Bad move!

Be bold enough to have it in the open where everyone can see it and make it eye level. I'm not talking Lebron James eye level either. If you need to move some things around in the service area, do so. Remember, this is to help build long-term habits that your team needs regardless, and the more they see it, the more the tips will help them with their next guest interaction.

Knowing your basic KPIs for your brand or restaurant is a skill for a good manager. Building on the layers of KPI levels through your organization and incorporating your team is the skillset of a great leader. It's not about working harder or being a mathematician; it's just knowing how to put numbers in real-world tactics for your team to execute.

The Takeaway

No matter what your Key Performance Indicators are, it is not enough to only know them. Learning how to make them make sense in your everyday routine and what areas of your business drive each one, directly or indirectly, helps you know how to move them.

Incorporating your team to track, meet, and exceed tasks that are relevant to those KPIs garners whole team ownership in moving those levers. Keep the steps to moving your KPIs simple and show them loudly and proudly. But don't make it a task or dashboard that will consume more of your time. Enlist your leaders on your team to find the information, post the data, and inform the rest of your team how everyone is doing.

KPIs are only beneficial when everyone (and I mean everyone) understands what each goal means, how it affects the customer, and the little things each team member does daily that helps swing them one way or another. Train it through orientation, make it a part of your 1-on-1s (chapter on that later), and have it visible with tips and tricks to meet and beat it.

The Angle

One unintended consequence to be aware of; when you focus on a KPI, lower skilled operators become single minded and may do things detrimental to the long-term health of the business to "get the number". You yourself need to know the "cheats" and create guardrails.

*-**Pat Peterson** - Senior VP of Restaurants, Wagamama USA, NY NY*

KPIs help align your team around what matters most and the measures that can quantify progress (or lack thereof) and provide a record of milestone goals and achievements. KPIs should be measured on an absolute basis and trends to see long term results.

*-**Kimberly Grant** – Fortune 100 Director, Performance Food Group, Washington DC*

Key performance indicators are essential to paving a pathway to desired results especially in an industry that requires constant multi-tasking and is often attempting to reach goals that can conflict with one another. Defining KPIs and clearly communicating a reasonable and attainable goal for each one not only keeps the organization focused on what matters most but helps balance opposing goals. For example, creating a KPI for labor/efficiency and a KPI for sales growth could be counterintuitive if both KPIs have an overly aggressive goal. However, if both are set with reasonable and balanced goals it will keep the organization from pushing too hard in one direction and ultimately damaging overall results.

KPIs with objectives properly selected, communicated clearly, and progress systematically shared, keep an organization focused through the multitude of distractions. In addition, clearly defined KPIs allow identification of progress and celebration of wins on the path to success which is critical to keeping the team engaged.

-**Paul Baldasaro** – *COO, Taco Mac, Atlanta GA*

Owner Like Orientation

The Main Course

This next chapter is one the most overlooked elements in creating the culture every manager and leader wants in their restaurant and organization. This foundation of culture value is so high, it is arguably the best ROI with new hires when performed correctly. That is executing an Owner Like Orientation.

An Owner Like Orientation is not just bringing someone onto your team that is focused on one position for the next few weeks or even months with hopes they branch out to more in the future. It's bringing them onboard to where they see the big picture of your business as a whole and being able to apply your company goals and meet customer expectations consistently on day one.

When implemented properly your current team will embrace new hires and work with them to hit current goals, not just shy away from the new hire because the learning curve feels burdensome.

Sometimes trainer burnout from turnover can diminish the value of passing on knowledge to a new hire as well. If higher than average turnover is your number one issue, I suggest engaging in one-on-ones sooner than later with your entire team to find out why employees are not just choosing to leave your company, but why the others have chosen to stay. Consistently high turnover will always takeaway the effectiveness of Owner Like Orientation.

Now, let's talk through the steps of performing this method. Each level doesn't have to be performed in its entirety, although performing all actions will greatly increase your chance of effectiveness. You can choose to lean on certain areas that match your business structure in varying degrees.

For example, you may not have the authority to increase how much onboarding is completed online instead of in-person, or you may not have control of the job descriptions through Indeed or Monster. But you can still apply the other 8 tactics that help support a stronger onboarding and orientation process.

To front load the 'how' of an Owner Like Orientation you must:

1. Define what working for you and your team is like in that role when advertising.
2. Include your team in the interview process.
3. Make the job offer formal and make their acceptance of the offer a big deal.
4. Find ways to stay connected with them to prepare them for their first day.
5. Make onboarding as digital as possible.
6. Schedule yourself to be organized and present for their first day.
7. Build your company goals, current business plan, and customer experience into the orientation process.
8. Involve current accomplishments to show where your team is heading.
9. Begin planning your one-on-one time with the new team member.
10. Lead them with the right mindset.

Let's walk through what each of the above looks like in your world.

Define the Role - as per usual, the beginning is usually where we drop the ball. Anyone can find the job description of a fry cook, sauté cook, or bar manager on any career search website and read what one does in that role. What they can't find is what it's like working that role in your four walls. This needs to written clearly and concisely in a section that is no longer than 30 seconds. Being as descriptive as possible within 30 seconds sounds challenging, but it is the most effective. You want to keep it short because the applicant will start to lose interest the longer the description. This 30 second read is only for the definition of this role in your four walls.

List the role definition in your four walls first, then list general responsibilities of the role in a second section, then brand or company specific information last. This layout will front load the information that directly targets the candidate first to see if this is a good fit to apply for.

Lastly, list the perks of working for your company and don't be afraid to include pay rate and bonus potential if it applies. Nothing is more frustrating or time consuming than scheduling an interview, making a connection, then finding out the pay rate expectations was not in the same ball park let alone on the same planet. Level-setting in the description helps to reduce that possibility.

Include Your Team - now, I'm not suggesting a group interview with one interviewee and three interviewers. I am however suggesting that your strongest right or left-hand assistant that is adept in soft skills, and active in the training process, is the first or second to interview all candidates.

Including your team in the process helps to build culture internally on feeling valued, and externally by giving the candidate the opportunity to speak with someone that is only a few steps ahead of them. It increases the team morale and buy in from your trainers and/or assistants that helped to interview them when training. It also paints the picture of team growth and ownership to the applicant insuring they won't just be another cog in a machine and that their opinion is important for the entire organization.

Your assistant should also be the first to interview all candidates. When the general or store manager interviews first, gives their opinion to the assistant manager, then passes them along for the second interview, the assistant is more likely to agree with the preconceived notions of their boss. Not all assistants are that easily swayed by their bosses first impressions on a candidate, but many more are than not. By letting them interview first you're able to use this process as a continued development and the both of you can calibrate more effectively on what is good candidate is by position needed.

If your assistant needs coaching on what questions to ask during the interview process, give them 3-5 questions that are fitting for that role and have them begin with those first. Be sure they write down the interviewee's answers to those questions during the interview for reference. As your assistant gets more comfortable and questions expand, continue to have them write the questions and answers for the candidate. This way when they see a great, or not so great, hire come through they can learn from the Q&A's from prior interviews to more easily spot potential candidates in the future. Remember, ABC - Always Be Coaching!

Make it Formal - some of the most exciting and stressful times in one's life are getting married, making a large purchase, and starting a new job. What makes it more or less exciting is the build up to the big day being stressful and unsure of your decisions, or something that was given support and confirmation that everything is going to be wonderful. By making a formal offer you help set the tone that you are serious about your possible new hires career and professional development. When making an offer quickly, and in a roundabout way, it makes the candidate feel like they are not that important or even a quality investment in your time or theirs. With ongoing labor challenges, we all understand the need to be nimble, move quickly, and get an offer to a potential candidate. The way we can help improve this is by making the offer formal.

First, have a script memorized that makes it easy to fill in information for both you and the candidate during the interview process. Below is a script found on Indeed's Career Guide for one to use, edit, and make their own:

"Mike, I enjoyed getting to know you during your interview process, and I think you'd make an impressive addition to [Company name]'s. We interviewed [Number of candidates] candidates for the [Position name] position, but based on your [Experience or skill 1], [Experience or skill 2], and [Experience or skill 3], you're the person we want for the team. I think [Reason 1] and [Reason 2] really make you the top candidate."

"I'm excited to offer you this position with a base/hourly salary of [Salary amount] and other benefits like [Notable benefit 1], [Notable benefit 2] and [Notable benefit 3]. I will send you an official offer package later today, but I wanted to share the good news with you right away. What do you think?"

Some keys in doing this correctly are:

1. Show authentic excitement.
2. Tell them why they were chosen to receive the offer.
3. Give them the compensation amount.
4. Get a response from them.

In the end, it's all about the formal presentation and the feeling that candidate gets that this is the right decision. When we think about the opposite approach, of finishing an interview, confirming their availability, then making a short offer, the candidate can feel like they're not fully committed to the job before they even start. Below is an approach we may have said or witnessed too often:

"Mike, thanks for coming in today. I really enjoyed the interview. I want to go ahead and give you an offer for $12 an hour to work [Company name]'s. Orientation is next Tuesday at 9:00 am. What do you think?"

You can tell the second approach sets a much lower expectation of what a career may look like in your company, and leaves lots of questions about why this would be considered as a right fit. Setting the tone early with a formal offer for a dishwasher or a Maître d' helps to reaffirm the first steps into a new professional relationship.

<u>Stay Connected</u> - staying Connected is the perfect segue from Make it Formal. After making an offer then receiving the acceptance there is always a deafening silence to follow for days or even weeks to come. Kind of like asking your partner to marry you, them saying yes, then drive home 6 hours from a long-distance vacation with no conversation. Awkward.

After an emotional roller-coaster of committing to a new position with a new company, don't leave gravity to its own and bring down your new hire's elation. This can be very similar to buyer's remorse for some if left without weekly affirmations of one's choice. Instead of using paperwork as a 'stay connected' point, use other affirmations to help the new employee stay excited about their upcoming first day. A Welcome Kit email with information about the history of the brand or owner is a good start. This helps to give depth to the company's roots.

A great idea is a welcome video with messages from people within the organization. Again, keep this short and sweet as well. Another idea is welcome swag in 2-3 separate mailings and packages. The first package can be fun swag with a tee shirt, mug, and stationary items. The next kit can be books on self-development or books written about the company culture. Lastly, a package with information of names and pictures to those that are on their team, as well as list of acronyms your company uses that others may not know. Do you remember how frustrating your first month was when everyone around you was using words you never heard of before and you had to nod your head in agreement as if you knew what they were talking about? How about when you walked in and took you a week just to learn the names of everyone you work with? Frustrating!

Whether calling once a week, texting to check on the upcoming new hire, sending welcoming packages, or the list of who their team is. All of these can be great touch points before your new hires first day that helps to reaffirm their choice of choosing you as a new employer, and raises the chances of them staying.

<u>Make it Digital</u> - one of the largest turnoffs on the first day for any new hire is the monotony of filling out loads of paperwork, by hand. In today's digital times businesses should be well equipped to have an option for new hires to do most of their onboarding paperwork through a portal. This saves countless

hours and mistakes in order to make sure the focus on the first day is acclimation to a new team, not acclimation to a W-4.

This is also one of the categories that you may not have much control over. If you don't, then try to stay organized in how much time is used in completing this portion on site. Mistakes on forms or having to fill out forms that have been misplaced takes away from the overall onboarding and orientation experience.

<u>Be Organized & Present</u> - imagine getting all hyped and excited about your very first day at work: the interview was amazing, you were able to meet some really cool people. You got the offer you were wanting and expecting, and your new workplace even sent you a welcome package with some swag and history about the company.

Your family has been so sick and tired of hearing you bragging about everything your new job has done for you that they can't wait to get you out the door. Secretly though, they are happy that the value they've always seen in you someone else sees and appreciates, giving you an opportunity to further your success.

You get to work 20 minutes early in your Monday-best, stride on in, and await the fireworks welcome. Then, you walk in and your new boss forgot today was orientation. Or, she remembered today was your first day but a big meeting came up and now she is running late, leaving you in the lobby by yourself for the next hour. You can hear the air being let out the proverbial balloon.

As you would imagine your goal is to have the focus on being organized and present for their first day as you want them to be every day in their new position. This is not a good to have. This is a must do. Cell phone put away. Emails on pause. Someone in charge as you're out of pocket. And everything laid out in order that it needs to be completed in. Showing this dedication to your new team member will reciprocate 100% every single time.

This day is the very start of the activation period. Plan for it, celebrate, involve the entire team, make it personable and give them a view of the company they joined, not just one position. If the first day of activation/onboarding does not go well, it is hard to fully recover.

Show Them the Big Picture - Think about how you usually bring someone onboard your restaurant or hotel. You check the schedule to see when they should be arriving. Get a table ready with their first set of uniforms, paperwork, and other information. You greet them in the lobby, ask them if they want something to drink, then bring them over to the table to begin and recite your 12 commandments. After the pen runs hot from all the scribbling and signing, you then give them a mini tour, put them on a laptop for some computer-based training, and maybe introduce to them to their new station or position.

Although this is what we've done for years, this is probably the worst way to bring on a new hire. When you think about it, you are subconsciously teaching them that when they walk in the door for the next few weeks or even months, the only thing that they should be concerned with is their new break table, a computer screen, and that position.

Think about it. Have you noticed that the same table you do orientation somehow becomes their break table?

A better approach is to give a tour of your business through the guest's eyes, starting from the curb. Remember, this is how your customers view your business. They see it from the road, in a vehicle as they are passing by, and they view the whole thing. Walk them around the exterior pointing out what they may or may not see that adds to the guest experience or takes away from it.

When the exterior is complete, enter the doors and talk through the sight lines of what every customer sees as they walk in. Is it trash cans? Clutter? Open Spaces? Team Members?

As your walking them through, describe what a 1-, 3-, or 5-star service is for that area, view, or even interaction is, with 1 being the lowest and 5 the highest. Now you're also training them to make a connection with your company's guest feedback scores, and what their contribution is to that feedback being strong or having room for improvement.

During one-on-one coaching sessions, I help leaders create custom orientation walk through's designed for their business, customer, and locations.

Doing this owner like orientation, a few things begin to click for the new addition to your team. They now look at the building much differently knowing that they can have an impact on the business from when they pull up, not just once in position. When they are in guest areas, not just on the service line. They also get a numerical understanding of what sub-par, par, and above par service and/or cleanliness is. All on the first day of orientation.

Depending on the size and layout of your business, this will add an additional 15-25 minutes to your usual orientation but will give you and your team a return that lasts their entire time under your leadership. Your return on investment will be miles above what you usually get now.

Think about the level of trust your team has with a new hire that comes onboard with a heightened execution and understanding of the big picture. This one step helps to rebuild some of that trust and connection some managers have lost with new teams.

Show Them the Way - To answer your question, yes, I am a Mandalorian fan! 'The way' I am referring to is showing your new team member some of the recent accomplishments by your team and brand.

When you think about the Oxford definition of orientation it is - 'the determination of the relative position of something or someone'. It is hard to get that if you don't know where something or someone recently came from or where it is headed. Use examples of goals set in sales building, customer satisfaction metrics, or even cost savings over the last week, month, or quarter. This underlines the fact that the business doesn't just focus on a shift-to-shift survival, but a well thought out target and plan to hit that target that everyone is involved in.

In this sense the new team member gets the orientation and direction of their immediate team that they will be working beside. By sharing recent accomplishments of the team, it gives the new hire a sense of where the attention and focus has been headed. This can be shared during the big picture walk through of your building, or in one of the Welcome Kits sent to the new hire as a reading reference. This will again enhance their orientation before they set foot in the building.

Engage with One-on-Ones - Even before you hit the first quarterly or biannual review, you should be mapping out your new team members one-on-ones. Now, some may call me extreme, but I wholly believe that O3s (one-on-ones) should be conducted weekly with your entire team. I do however understand that bandwidth will determine hitting that goal or not consistently. Whatever your interval is, the O3 should be conducted with the next round you have scheduled.

Doing so sets aside time for you to get to know your new hire better and what their goals are. Notice I did not say it gives you more time to catch up on things they need to complete for their onboarding. Please refer to Key #3 on how to correctly engage in O3s for further explanation.

The helps lay the groundwork for a long professional relationship to identify and address challenges, give feedback, and help the team grow in their roles. The best time to start is on day one.

Lead with The Right Mindset - As you go through the transitions of marketing for the open role, interviewing, sending offers, prepping for orientation and onboarding, then to training, and finally development, it's important to remember to wear the right hats as a leader. In Key #5 we discuss Leading with The Right Mindset: Managing vs Leading vs Coaching and the fact that hospitality leaders will act within all three mindsets multiple times per day. The challenge is knowing which one to use to reach the best outcome, not just a positive outcome.

Working through the progressions in an Owner Like Orientation you see where most start in a Leadership Mindset by painting the picture of what success in this open role looks like. They shift to a Coaching Mindset in the interview process as they master the one-on-one environment and dive deep into the goals of the candidate. The Managing Mindset is in full swing during the offer and prep for orientation stages. This continues as you think through the parameters and budgets while staying organized. The training and development stage will shift most into multiple mindsets depending on the situation. With all of the mental movements, being conscious of what mindset you're in helps you reach your desired outcome.

The Takeaway

The goal of an Owner Like Orientation is to have the excitement of joining your team last beyond the accepting of an offer. To do that we have to consciously extend that excitement beyond the first 90 days of working with us by creating phases in the onboarding and orientation. Orientation can be viewed as an event that helps to welcome an employee into your business and get them pointed in the same direction the rest of your team is heading in. Onboarding can be viewed as series of events and trainings that helps a new employee become successful in their role.

No matter which of two you are executing, the secret is sharing as much relevant information as possible to help the new hire feel they made right choice, help them connect with their new team, and be able to see the big picture of the company as a whole, not just a position. When this happens you get a higher return on investment for a new employee and your team is much happier training someone that sees the big picture.

First, define and demonstrate what their life would be like working for your business. Then, make an enthusiastic offer in a formal setting and tell them the reason why they are a great fit. If you can't think of three reasons why, are they actually the right fit? Next, find ways to stay connected with the new hire by whatever means of communication they are most comfortable with. Send them information that answers the most common questions one has on the first week of any new job without making it seem like homework.

Then make onboarding digital so that the first day is productive, not a mountain of paperwork and signatures. On the first day give them the tour through the guest's eyes and through your team's eyes, painting the big picture that connects them to the parts of the business that makes their role successful. Start planning your one-on-one engagement early on so they get in the same rhythm as the rest of your team to get and give feedback, and explore ideas on continuing their development. Finally, lead with the right mindsets of managing, leading and coaching as you create an environment for success on their new journey.

All of these steps are great at enhancing your current onboarding and orientation process, but all of them are not necessary. You have the ability to choose which one fits better for your culture and team. I do however suggest you choose at least one, execute it consistently and fully, then measure the return you get from making your team better on day one.

The Angle

Empathy is the most important tool in my toolbox. Looking at a situation from someone else's perspective completely changes how I respond to them. During onboarding and orientation, my focus is on understanding the employee's current situation. This enables me to put them at ease, ask questions, and make them comfortable through the process.

*   **-Julie Thompson** – *Senior Instructional Design, Zaxby's Grill, Atlanta GA*

Each member of the management team is responsible for weekly check ins with the new team member. The GM maybe responsible for the first 30 days, the KM may have as their Area of Responsibility the next 30 days and so on so the new team member is set for succeed along the way.

*   **-Gerald Pulsinelli** – *CEO, Viva Chicken, Charlotte NC*

I truly believe that onboarding is an art. Each new employee brings with them a potential to achieve and succeed. To lose the energy of a new hire through poor onboarding is an opportunity lost.

-Sarah Wetzel – *Director of Human Resources, engage:BDR*

The importance of onboarding is significantly increased these days since the average turnover at work is less than four years and lifetime employment strategies are out of date.

-Reid Hoffman, Ben Casnocha and Chris Yeh – *Authors of "The Alliance"*

We want to focus on creating a memorable experience for the new hire in the first year rather than processing them in the first few weeks.

-Cheryl Hughey – *Director of Onboarding, Southwest Airlines*

"…the biggest reason why people fail or underperform has to do with the culture and politics of the organization…so I focus a lot on basically three things: how we are going to help this person adapt to the new culture; how are we going to connect them to the right people and help them form the right relationships; and how are we going to be sure that we really align expectations in every direction so that they're set up for success…"

-Michael Watkins – *Author, "The First 90 Days"*

Delegate By Creating Mini-GMs

The Main Course

Keeping your business in order with all the checklists, multiple orders, food safety issues, training programs, and new menu rollouts is about as chaotic as it can get in our world. Not only do you have to be a master of many hats, you must be a master of many hands.

What's the answer to this daily conundrum? Simply increase the number of heads and hands by developing mini-General Managers on your team to help make the steady increases of processes not just work, but thrive with success.

Although honestly, creating mini-GMs is a step that is harder than it sounds, with a few major challenges to overcome.

The first challenge: trust. You have to admit it – you don't trust that the person working under you can do the tasks you do and produce the same results. If so, they would be a manager too, right? Or, you may not trust that you will get enough credit when they do it correctly as you're fighting to increase your own net worth and value. If the second reason is your largest trust concern, then you may be halfway out the door already.

I'm sure it's a fact that every schedule you ever wrote was on budget with no holes (yeah right…), every truck order was perfectly placed (really?), and all your inventories included every grain of salt in the building. SMH… of course, you've been perfect since your rookie days in training. But in all honesty, it's just not true. The human brain has a natural protective function that makes one forget many traumatizing situations, especially those with regret, and replaces those with memories of success and gratification. Hence your memory of perfection on your way to the top.

The second challenge is, who the heck has the time or budget to train someone? Have you seen your labor budget lately? Because no one else has. Let us not forget the very first Key in this book is knowing your KPIs! Training is not something that is allotted for only the first 7 days someone comes on board as a new hire. It never stops, even up to the day one leaves for their next role.

You Never. Stop. Training.

It's just some managers structure their team to keep training going, and some do not.

The culmination of both challenges makes delegating nearly impossible and downright difficult. In this chapter, we'll explore ways to map out what can be delegated, who to delegate to, and why it would be a great idea to take it off your plate. By the end of this chapter, you will have a solid foundation to start to train mini-GMs in your business.

The first step is to figure out exactly what you do as manager/GM every day. This is where the truth in the monotony on paper may end up killing you. Typically, whenever someone is told to delegate their duties, they think about big ticket items or items they don't like doing, like inventory, truck orders, payroll, line checks, HR issues, etc. The trick to delegation isn't passing off the large duties. It's taking the time to write down all the minute items in one's day, week and month that takes up some time, but repetitiously can add up to several wasted hours a month.

For example, here's a list of daily/weekly tasks that restaurant managers have but, in most organizations, doesn't have to be done by the GM:

Follow up on Caterings

Daily Produce Order

Line Check

Waste Sheet

Assign Daily Detail List

Assign Weekly Detail List

Sidework Chart

Respond to Social Media Compliments/Complaints

R&M Follow Up

Coordination of Training and Cross training

When looking at this list it seems manageable to just pick a few things and let Brittany know that she is now the 'Queen of Waste Sheets'. If only it was that simple, my friend, because timing is everything. Meaning that all your duties need to have time frames for completion with them. This is to help us know the impact of what passing this off to someone else means in the value of time taken out of their daily routine and to define the time expectation in which you feel it should be completed. Nothing rocks your boat harder than passing off a task that would take you 10-15 minutes to complete and takes Brittany 30-40 minutes to get done.

Next, you need to define the frequency in which it is completed.

Doing this helps to clarify whether it can be given to one individual (monthly/weekly) or to a certain position that is scheduled during the day (daily/multiple times daily). It may make more sense to assign a certain duty to the PM line opener, or the BOH closer each night because that position is always staffed.

In the next two steps, you should give each task a Priority Level and an Administrative Level. Giving your team a clear picture of what should be done first, second, and so on, will help clear the headache that happens when the right things are being done at all the wrong times.

I'm sure you can recall examples of your team completing duties at the worst possible time during a shift but was still a task that had to be completed before the end of day.

In order to organize your tasks by Priority Level, I suggest listing three categories:

1. Must be done above all other tasks and has a hard deadline.

2. Important, with a deadline, but not urgent.

3. Important, but no deadline, and no immediate effect to business if not completed.

If you notice all three Priorities are important. If they weren't, they wouldn't be on your task list. Also, all three show that you do need to complete them. Even Priority Level 3 can include taking the cash deposit for the day. You can argue that some organizations want this taken every day and some even twice a day. Will guests stop coming in or the lights turn off if you don't take it first? No. But it still needs to get done, although there won't be an immediate effect on business if not completed. That doesn't mean you won't lose your job in some cases...

The best way to organize these priorities is to think about which items that, if not completed, would have an immediate negative impact on your guest. If your customer walked away with a negative experience because that item was not complete, you are most likely looking at a Priority 1 item.

These items can also be classified as items that are on another person's or company's deadline. For example, truck or product orders that have items needing to be ordered to get to your business on time. Since the timeline is not in your control and it would affect your customer in the near future, this would also be considered as Priority 1.

An example of Priority 2 would be checking emails. Many master-level consultants would argue that this would not be a priority at all. Depending on your business type, that answer can vary. Even for restaurants, the number of online orders that come through email, including catering orders, is a significant amount of your total sales. Failing to ever check email communications throughout the day in any industry leaves many leaders in the dark about the ever-changing initiatives and (non)emergencies being rolled down to your building. Is checking email important, absolutely. The point is that the Priority Level would not be higher than unlocking the doors, prepping your cash sales systems, or performing quality checks on your products to make sure it is ready for your guests. It does still need to be done throughout the day with importance on execution dependent on the communication.

For Administrative Levels, I suggest these categories:

1. GM/MP Only

2. Assistant Manager/Shift Leader

3. Core Employee

In this case I define a Core Employee as someone who has tenure in your organization, has shown a heightened sense of responsibility, and has earned trust among your leadership team. The other 2 Admin Levels are self-spoken for.

Now comes the task of putting it all into a functioning list that you can begin planning on how to delegate out to your team. The figure below shows how one group has taken this exercise to the next level.

Daily

Item	Priority Level	Admin Level	Time	Day(s)
Check Deposit/Count Safe	1	2	10-15 min	Daily
Bank Run/Change Order	2	2	20-30 min	M-Sat
Check Caterings	1	3	5-10 min	Daily
Complete Line Chart	2	2	2-3 min	Daily
Check Emails	2	2	2-3 min	Daily
Produce Order	1	3	5-7 min	Sun, T, Th
Input Invoices	2	1	10-15 min	M, W, Sat
Line Check	1	3	20-30 min	Daily
Pre Shift Meeting	2	2	5 min	Daily
Open/Mid/Close checklist	2	2	10-15 min ea	Daily
End of day paperwork	1	2	20-30 min	Daily
Recap Manager Log	2	2	5 min	Daily
Waste Sheet	3	3	2-3 min	Daily
Assign detail cleaning duties	2	2	2-3 min	Daily
Catering Follow Ups	3	2	5-10 min	A/N

This clearly sets the stage on the task to be performed, what should be completed in order of priority, how long it should take to complete the task, and the frequency in which it's done. All that's missing is putting the name of the individual beside each task, how long the task will be assigned to the individual (for continued development) and even what time of day to do them.

What one can begin to realize is how few items are truly 'GM/MP Only' tasks unless directly instructed by the GMs immediate supervisor. For the restaurant manager who believes they are the only one to complete administrative duties daily, they are carving out at least 3.5 hours out of the precious 10-hour shift to complete the duties shown above. You can imagine the lost time in people development, community engagement, guest building and more that is replaced with tasks that more than one person is capable of successfully completing with the right training. Now add on the weekly, monthly, and quarterly tasks to the list above and the extra time now found in a month shows how much this change to delegation needs your immediate attention.

Next, we must successfully train each duty to a leader on our team. Let me back up for a second. Everything on the list you've created doesn't need to be farmed out to someone on your team. Delegating duties should encompass items that directly impact the individual you wish to delegate to and/or help the individual to be a more productive part of the leadership team.

For example, you wouldn't delegate the Produce Order, Line Check, and Waste Log to a Front of House employee. Their involvement in the overall processes of Back of House procedures would be very little to none. You also wouldn't train completing Pre-Shift Meetings to someone who has not expressed interest in becoming a manager in the future. The delegated duties must make sense for the persons development path they are on and/or for their overall impact on the things that duty effects.

You can also add this in as an additional column letting your team know what days they will be trained on these duties and when it will officially be theirs to own. To start, I suggest only delegating three tasks per person. Anything more than that can be an overload for them and yourself.

When training, include the 'Whys' behind every task. There's a more definitive chapter on this later in the book. But the key here is to make sure that you are allotting time to properly train your team on new tasks by using the Tell, Show, Do, Review & Follow Up technique of teaching.

Now that you've mastered prioritizing and delegating some of your daily duties in your restaurant, let's look at how you can create mini-GMs to help with the backbone of development with your teams.

Just to be clear, development isn't just training. It's a culmination of the understanding, skillset, and execution in any area of your business.

With this I also suggest sticking with three areas. Culinary (Kitchen), Service (FOH, Bar, Host) and Guest Relations (Marketing/Social Media). If you're applying the principles of this book correctly, the next level of this is teaching your Culinary Manager how to split up his/her department into three areas where she has a mini-GM for different categories as well (BOH Training Mini-GM, Equipment & Food Safety Mini-GM, and Food Cost & Waste Mini-GM). For Service, it could be FOH Training, Bar Training, & Host Training. And for Guest Relations – Rewards Program Sign Ups, Social Media Updates/Responses, & LSM Marketing. You get the idea.

A clear picture of what their role is needs to be defined and understood by everyone on your team. It's not enough to just have a person that is head of 'Local Store Marketing' to seem like you are advanced in your team development skills. Your goals, budgets and KPIs must reflect their ownership in that category. It's also great idea to consider giving them a portion of a Bonus that's tied directly to that KPI if they are a large part of meeting and beating those goals.

To round out your team, change out their responsibilities every 3-6 months. As others see employees gaining more responsibility and possibly having a part of a bonus pool for certain categories, you'll see more of your team wanting to learn more about the business and take ownership in key areas. You will also find certain stars that will standout to teach other team members what they learned and tips and tricks to help complete the task at a higher level.

With this increased responsibility comes important duties and reporting. Your team that you have delegated to will have to report up to you weekly or as needed to keep you ahead of relevant information. They will also be involved, or in charge, of any new rollouts or projects in their area of responsibility as well. This should be covered in your weekly 1-on-1s, again, more to come on that later.

Lastly, all these items must come with some type of empowerment that is very clear to the rest of the team. No one wants to have responsibility with no real empowerment in getting things done. Put the rails of restraints up of what they can and cannot do and let them run it to a higher plane of success. One person concentrating on 3 specific tasks and duties is much more effective than one GM focusing on 300.

The Takeaway

Your duties will never stop multiplying as long as you're in an industry that thrives on driving results to a customer base that has many options with your competitors, and a profit line with slim margins. You will get more data to pour over, reports to fill out, areas to monitor, technology to incorporate, and less time to do so. If it deals with Sales & Profits, Guest Service Scores, Team Development and Food Safety, you may as well call these your main 4 pillars or B.I.G. Rocks.

Everything else that just drives you crazy, but you know you still must keep an eye on it, you can call your whirlwind. Developing leaders to help you control the whirlwind first is key as you have more influence in driving the levers that move your Wildly Important Goals (WIGs).

Define what your B.I.G. Rock & whirlwind items are and list them by Priority and Administrative level to see what can be delegated. Put expected completion times and frequency of when it needs to be done with each task. Finally, put names with each task (2-3 per person max), date of training and date of ownership. Follow up with them weekly 1-on-1s to track progress, hurdles, and success stories.

Give your team depth by changing tasks every 3-6 months or when you feel the team member is ready to take on additional responsibility. Instead of layer on more, simply swap item responsibilities with other on your team ready for development and incorporate the team member exiting the task in teaching the next one how to complete it.

Delegating is one of the core steps of my Manage Leader Coach Model. All book owners are eligible to receive a free Delegation template so you can lead your team with whole team ownership mindset, instead of lead alone. Just email me at jbrooks@jasonebrooks.com and use the subject 'Free Delegation Template' to receive yours at no cost.

The Angle

Delegating is one of the most important elements of leadership that is often overlooked. In most cases, people want to be given the opportunity to succeed and delegation allows that. I have found that by focusing on the individual project and how to delegate with it instead of a holistic person and their workload, you can be much more effective of a leader. Some projects, delegation has to be direct, while others you can be looser with based on the experience of the team being delegated to. (i.e The One Minute Manager)

*-**Alan Magee** – VP Marketing & Communications, Empire Portfolio Group, NY NY*

The art of delegating successfully is something that most learn over time. I like to break it down to a few simple checkpoints. Aptitude, Time & Desire. The individual you are working with must portray the aptitude, talent or even reach potential to successfully fulfill the task at hand otherwise it is doomed to fail right from the start. Secondly and probably the most important step is to evaluate if this person has the time to execute the task. To many times we don't look at this piece when delegating and wonder why potentially our "go to" team member failed at meeting our expectations. Finally, is desire. Choosing projects or tasks that interest that team member helps leverage the probability of getting the desired outcome. Take the extra time it takes to walk through these steps and there is less chance of having to return to repair the outcome.

*-**Paul Baldasaro** – COO, Taco Mac, Atlanta GA*

Delegation is absolutely essential the further you progress within an organization. This allows much more work to be completed, but equally as important, it allows people to develop their skills and the organization to have a greater level of buy-in on decisions and initiatives.

*-**Paul Macaluso** – President & CEO, Another Broken Egg, Atlanta GA*

On a Side Note:

Sit Down for All Your Conversations

Our industry is fast paced, quick thinking and always on your feet, which makes us one of the most adaptable out there. We can comprehend multiple conversations going on around us, distinguish sounds of alarms and timers from other like sounds, and predict the next 20 minutes into a shift according to the current situation with crystal-ball-like accuracy. The challenge to that is just as quickly as all these points of information are coming onto our radar, they are just as quickly falling off it. Just as quickly as it happens to us, it happens to those that work beside and report directly to us. Yet still sometimes we believe that in the middle of all this (controlled) chaos that as we give feedback to help improve efficiency and throughput, our teams take that feedback and store it in a steel trap. Hogwash.

Let's take a look at a more relaxed environment. You're walking by someone that's on your team during down time and you give them feedback about something that's been your mind about their development. You have the right authoritative stance, the firm but caring eye contact, and the Morgan Freeman tone that reverberates through any room. After those 3 minutes of a deep conscientious like dive into the golden words that will make them a better human, you walk away knowing you nailed it and should clock out for the rest of week as the universe is now back in alignment. Hogwash.

Whether it's a war like environment, or one with the perfect LED lighting and piano solo, standing on the line giving feedback to your team only carries you but so far. Everything in their average day happens to them happens while standing on the line. Mentally it's hard to consciously differentiate what is more important than the other for most people in that same environment.

Now, I'm not stating that no feedback should be given in the middle of a shift. As a matter of fact, you're very close to the chapter on giving feedback like a leader. Great leaders know this is a must to help correct things as the day evolves. Great leaders also know that recapping the day in a controlled setting helps to emphasize specific points because the person across from you has your full attention. This is the power of making words stick.

What this does is take the listener out of the element of paying attention to everything, and just paying attention to the conversation at hand. Naturally, any sit-down conversation makes one feel more at attention because they feel something is deftly important and needs all of their focus.

Engage with One-on-Ones

The Main Course

Do you remember that strange sunken feeling you sometimes get in your gut around the end of the fiscal year when you have to give a review to one of your subordinates and you know it's not going to well? Maybe it will go well, but they fight along every line of feedback you give them through the process. Or, it doesn't go well, and you have to call in a small swat team to escort them away from the table as they refuse to sign their evaluation.

Do you know what that means? That you're probably doing a poor job at managing your people, and you're definitely not leading them. They have tasks, duties, and areas of responsibilities, but for some reason you two are not on the same PLANET when it comes to their performance and your expectations of their performance on a daily or weekly basis.

The best way to insure you and your direct subordinates are on the same page is by conducting 1-on-1s.

Every single week.

You can exhale and roll your eyes all you want, but if you want to be successful at knowing your directs and getting high performance outputs from them even when you're not around, performing real 1-on-1s weekly is the only way to get you and your team where you want to be.

I know there is a group of you saying, "My team knows exactly where we are with each other. I'm in constant communication with them about everything that's going on with the company that will affect them."

That's a decent start to a midway point of where you want to be. It's true, you are in constant communication with them, but that communication is you telling them what's going on, what to do next, what not to do, and so forth. A continual one-way street with a few yellow lights for Tom Sullivan nods.

How many times a week do you set aside time for them to unload on you? Not just unload but contribute through communications on things that are on the top of their mind, not just yours.

One reason that your team may not do that is that they don't have the time to get a word in edgewise and, they most likely have been programmed that way indirectly because of your management style. And yes, it is important for them to let you know what's going on in their world because that's the key to collaboration and success. Your assistants and supervisors are a direct line to the vein of what is going on in the building.

Before we get started, I must give a lot of credit for the base of this chapter to Mark Horstman and Michael Auzenne of Manager Tools out of Burke, Virginia. Their informational podcasts and seminars have sparked and sharpened some of the greatest leaders in Fortune 1000 companies around the world. From their Manger Tools & Career Tools podcast to their online Roadmap to becoming a better leader, I highly suggest you invest some time to enjoy some of their wise words and priceless principles for leaders just like you.

With that said, let's lay down some non-negotiables for giving great 1-on-1's.

1. One on ones are to be scheduled just like clocking in. It's on a viewable schedule for both parties to see, acknowledge and plan their day around.

2. One on ones are never to be missed. Barring severe illness or death in the family, these do not get overlooked or overbooked. The minute you start missing them is the moment your team feels you no longer care about their professional well-being.

3. The number one focus is on them. No, this does not mean the whole time *you* are talking about *them*. This is the time for you to speak 35% of the time and they speak 65% of the time.

4. This leads into the next point, when you schedule 1-on-1s, make it for 30 minutes. The first 10 minutes are for them to talk to you about whatever topic they want. Family, kids, school, vacation plans, anything that is professionally appropriate that will get you to know them better. The other 10 minutes are for you, and I suggest you use this to follow up on topics they may have brought up at the last 1-on-1. The final 10 minutes are reserved for them to speak about career, growth and development topics.

5. Next, take notes, handwritten, not on a device. Typing

on a device makes the 1-on-1 feel like a deposition. Handwriting notes adds to the authentic sense of the meeting.

6. Which leads into another non-negotiable, No Devices. For you or them. Leave it in the office if necessary, but do not have them on you at all. Devices have trained us to divert our attention away from what we are currently doing to check notifications to see if it is more important than our current task. Nothing is more important during this time.

Those are 6 non-negotiables to help you perform more effective 1-on-1s.

The best place to hold these are somewhere that is not public. These discussions are solely between you and your subordinate. If you have an office with a door then in the office with the door closed. If not, then at a table in closed section where others do not walk by. If you have to hold these offsite, then you can, but I suggest staying on premise when possible.

When preparing yourself for a 1-on-1 always take time to review your notes from your previous meeting. Is there anything you were supposed to follow up on? If so, make sure you remain committed to getting that information before the next 1-on-1.

During the segment that you have 10 minutes to ask questions, you should plan on what you really want to communicate. Are there behaviors of theirs that you want to address? Are there organizational changes that are upcoming or have taken place recently? Was there a meeting you just attended with information you wanted to share?

Leading back to Non-Negotiable #3, try not to stray into questions and topics that are another data-dump. If the question or topic can be relayed at a different time or in a group communication, don't ask it during this precious time. If the communication is something that should be delivered person to person, you can take a few moments to cover.

Besides giving great information and updates, you should also think about positive feedback you can give during this time. This is a huge opportunity to build a stronger relationship between you both professionally. With the positive feedback, you can also give corrective feedback on past events to make sure they address future situations differently. Lastly, when planning what you want to communicate, you can also review something you want to delegate whether be it project, task, or work that's helpful in their development.

When you first start 1-on-1s, the communication juices don't always begin flowing right away. It will usually take you asking some effective questions and multiple meetings to get your team to open up to you. For example:

Tell me about what you've been working on?

What's your week been like?

Tell me about your family/weekend/activities?

What updates do you have on project x?

Are there any areas of your work that you're feeling confident about?

Are there any suggestions you have to make our next rollout more effective?

What are your thoughts on the most recent changes at work?

What are your future goals?

How do you plan to get to those goals?

What can you/we do differently next time?

These are all questions that can help your team begin to make 1-on-1s helpful for you and them and keep collaborations and contributions open and flowing instead of the usual day-to-day data dumps.

When taking notes as I stated before, you want to make sure that you take handwritten notes. No one on your team is going to believe that you have a photographic memory of all conversations and can sit down as they open up professionally about their development and you remember everything that was said. You should be setting the stage for taking everything they are saying into consideration as well as writing down information to follow up on for them. You should also have prewritten updates you want to make sure you mention as well.

Below is great example of a 1-on-1 form you can use that I have found to be very effective. It lists the team members name, the location they're in, date, time, personal information, a notes section for the team member, a notes section and question staging area for the manager speaking, then finally a follow up and development section.

The above is an 8.5 x 11 format that is easy to use with a clipboard. There is also an option of a shortened version on a 4 X 6 index card that can be helpful in your pocket when needed as well.

Completing notes and following up is critical in both parties seeing that this time is well spent. Many conversations are lost in day-to-day interactions and communications in the heat of the shift. 1-on-1s provide the focused time and energy to collaborate between you and your team member (manager) to help develop clear and concise communications.

Scan and upload each one into their folders to help track progress of these communications.

I cannot emphasize enough the importance of making 1-on-1s with your directs a fundamental pillar of how you develop the relationship in and on your team. It's time well spent that's dedicated to get to know the person you rely on to make the right decisions even when you're not in the building. Lastly, it's essential time to get caught up on important things separate from the day-to-day whirlwind conversations that can get lost in the day.

The Takeaway

1-on-1s cannot be looked at as another useless weekly meeting. As a matter of fact, you will find that your time to handle items you feel are important will increase because of the reduction of fixing mistakes. The there is no substitute for 1-on-1s.

All readers are eligible to receive a free 1-on-1 template so you can help manage, coach, and lead your teams to higher success. Just email me at jbrooks@jasonebrooks.com and use the subject 'Free 1-on-1 Template' to receive yours at no cost. Just small a thank you for supporting my book and a way for me to give back to the industry that made me what I am today.

The Angle

Consistency, clarity and focus. Set the meeting a regular cadence and stick to it like glue. That way as things come up that frustrate or perplex them, they say to themselves in the moment "well we're going to chat on Tuesday, and we can talk about it then". Be clear in advance about how you'll spend time. It could be "Next week I want to talk KPIs" or "hey let's talk turnover on Monday". Doing that in advance helps them feel prepared and trusted. You want them to look forward to these, not dread them as "gotcha" sessions. Then it's simple.... focus. Shut off the phone, ignore the I-watch. Focus more on asking open ended questions than making statements. Get them talking, then listen intently. If you can actively listen, you get what you asked for and so much more. Your team needs to know that at that moment there is nothing more important than them, doesn't matter if it's 15 minutes or an hour. If you take that time now in a structured environment, it will actually save you a dozen messy interactions and phone calls in the field. The more direct reports you have, the more important this becomes.

*-**Pat Peterson** - Senior VP of Restaurants, Wagamama USA, NY NY*

An effective 1 on 1 only happens when there is two-way dialogue. Key steps I use in the process are simple but at times can be overlooked. I like to refer to it as P4. Purpose, Preparation, Presentation & Path. People's beliefs are driven by their experiences so remembering to follow through on all these steps improve the probability of desired impact. Purpose, one must have a clear understanding of the desired outcome before engaging in a 1 on 1. Preparation is developed based on that Purpose and Presentation me coincide with one's desired outcome. Path is the roadmap to achieve your Purpose and it is uber important at this point you validate clarity and commitment to the receiving party. This format can be used effectively in more than traditional 1 on 1s and I have found affective in accomplishing commitment and desired results.

*-**Paul Baldasaro** – COO, Taco Mac, Atlanta GA*

During a 1-on-1, I allow my employees to lead the conversation. This time is for them, not me. I listen, answer questions, and gain insight on their goals and needs.

*-**Julie Thompson** – Senior Instructional Design, Zaxby's Grill, Atlanta GA*

We break it down, in a People, Execution (operations), and Results process where it is the Manager's meeting and the supervisor is the listener. And the key as the leader is to ask one more question to help support the manager in their development.

*-**Gerald Pulsinelli** – CEO, Viva Chicken, Charlotte NC*

You can create a CADENCE OF ACCOUNTABILITY with your GMs by having a recurring 1-on-1 with them. The MOST IMPORTANT rule is to never cancel. This is a meeting that happens at the same time every week/month/quarter no matter what. Death, taxes and keeping the 1-on-1 meeting. The GM has a PRIMER that is a one-page document that has all of the most important metrics of the store on it. He/she fills out this PRIMER before the meeting. They do most of the talking. Let them lead by reporting out to you on their store metrics (mentioned above). In addition, the PRIMER has questions that prompts the GM to recite the yearly goals for that year and if they are on-track or off-track. There is another question that prompts the GM to discuss any challenges they are facing outside of their control? (ex: is there road construction happening outside of their store next week?) This meeting needs to happen at a non-peak time, on a non-peak day, to minimize distractions (ex: Every first Tuesday of the month at 3pm). After the meeting, ask them to give you a tour of their store.

  -Steve Taylor – Managing Member, CapQueen3 LLC, Charlotte NC

Leading With the Right Mindset

The Main Course

There are three distinct but interchangeable mindsets that, when applied appropriately, will allow you to be more successful in conversations, organizational challenges, and team development. We're going to navigate through their differences, advantages, and downfalls to help you begin your road to mastery of each one. We'll also look at why, even with effort and investment, many businesses are failing at leadership. Simply put, companies are not incorporating an approach that includes three mindsets when developing their people.

My journey, like yours, has brought me to walk along the path of a two-sided coin. On one side, great organizations lead by great people making impactful results. And the other side, companies that spiraled out of existence due to non-directional leadership. The learnings and observations from all these companies are the foundation of this approach.

We'll also define the differences in managing, leading, and coaching and how you can easily identify each one. Finally, I'll give you steps to apply the balance of all three to your personal and professional life today, so that you can be more successful in everything you do tomorrow.

Let's look at some statistics around leadership and management:

According to a workplace study done by Zippia - The Career Experts[1], 83% of organizations believe it is important to develop leaders at every level of the company, but only 5% of businesses have implemented leadership development at all levels.

When we think about leadership development, should it only be reserved to C-suite levels, or should all levels of our organization be invested in equally allowing multiple departments to attract and retain top talent, improve the bottom line, and drive execution on strategies for company success?

According to GoRemotely[2], 78% of business managers actively focus on engaging with their employees, but only 48% of employees view their company leadership as having "high quality engagement". Soft skills as a people leader are a factor that is overlooked by nearly every industry. When we think back to our first management role, most of us probably remember

---

[1] Zippia. "35+ Powerful Leadership Statistics [2023]: Things All Aspiring Leaders Should Know" Zippia.com. Jun. 29, 2023, https://www.zippia.com/advice/leadership-statistics//.

[2] GoRemotely. "22 Inspiring Leadership Statistics for a Successful 2023". Goremotely.net March 07, 2023. https://goremotely.net/blog/leadership-statistics/#:~:text=A%20whopping%2079%25%20of%20employees,director%20roles%20in%20the%20workplace.

being a good employee, then interviewing internally for a higher role, and because we were so good at what we did, we thought that we could naturally teach others to be as successful as we were.

Although we all have natural abilities that make us excel in certain areas, managing others in a high-quality setting isn't natural. It is learned. And while failure helps us make successful choices in the future, we lose talented people in the meantime because this soft skill isn't established quickly enough. The good news is more businesses are investing in leadership development at the beginning of a new people leader role, not just after trial by fire.

Of the $366 billion[3] spent globally, US businesses spend nearly $166 billion on leadership development a year. Yet still, 79% of employees quit due to a lack of appreciation from leadership. Even with all the financial investment in the world, it still comes down to communication.

As a leader, communication isn't just a vehicle for delivering information. The power of a leader's word holds more weight than when they were an individual contributor. Not only must one focus on clarity, confidence, and defining the clear path for the organization, leaders must find ways to value employee ideas, make recognition an actionable culture, and encourage high performance by reinforcing desired behaviors without top-down direction.

MDA's Training Study[4] completed in 2020 showed that 74% of employees feel micromanaged due to unnecessary activities at work given by their manager. This correlates with the same study showing that 58% of managers say they didn't receive any management training at all. It's crazy to believe half of

[3] Zippia. "35+ Powerful Leadership Statistics [2023]: Things All Aspiring Leaders Should Know" Zippia.com. Jun. 29, 2023, https://www.zippia.com/advice/leadership-statistics//.

[4] mdatraining. "Statistics on management development in the workplace". Mdatraining.com Jan 15, 2020. https://mdatraining.com/blog/4-statistics-on-management-development-in-the-workplace/

managers in the workplace received no training for their role.

But as we dig deeper, it's not that shocking. Again, thinking back to our own early experiences, we were typically promoted for how well we performed in our current role, not because of how effective we were at ensuring the results and production of the ones around us.

When we look at the statistics around coaching, it is almost the exact opposite of management and leadership findings.

According to Upcoach[5], globally in 2022, businesses have invested only $90 billion in coach training. Now, I say only like I have an extra $90 billion in my pocket. But this is far below the annual investment for leadership & management training. Only 28% of companies measure the ROI of coaching consistently. Of those that do measure coaching, 72% reported an increase in productivity. Sixty-three-percent of organizations reported higher revenue and income growth from their competitors. Multiple studies found that the ROI from coaching in business is much higher than any other form of development.

So why aren't more businesses investing in coaching? Because it is looked at as a training reserved for the top 1% of organizations. But coaching doesn't have to be an approach from an external specialist being applied to an executive. It is also the approach and vehicle we use to communicate and develop all teams.

All these statistics show the more we can invest in management, leadership, and coaching development the better our business can be, and the better we are at understanding what the differences between the three are, the higher our return on investment will be when we apply them correctly.

So, how do we recognize the differences between the three?

Let's look at the layman terms:

---

[5] UpCoach. "Coaching Statistics: A Curated List of The Most Insightful Stats". Upcoach.com Jun 17, 2022. https://upcoach.com/coaching-statistics-insightful-stats/

1. Managing (Manager): to handle or direct with a degree of skill.
2. Leading (Leader): a person who has commanding authority or influence.
3. Coaching (Coach): to instruct, direct, or prompt; to train intensively.

The average hospitality leader will act in all three facets multiple times a day to reach positive results for their team. The trick is knowing which mindset and approach is appropriate for the given situation. Where we can fail is when we subconsciously commit too much to one mindset versus balancing the three.

The Managing Mindset.

In a Managing Mindset, you understand the parameters your team must work in, and when and what targets to hit. You bring new employees onto your team with a big picture view of the whole building, not just one position. Once in position, you help expand their knowledge of the organization through delegated tasks that match their role and skill set. Then you follow up and engage through one on ones to help build a long-lasting relationship.

Some of us may not believe it, but we use a management style more than any other style throughout our workday. Most believe that the manager is the middleman between the senior leadership team and a group of employees. They are the main communication line and conduit that coordinates and executes the operational plans for company goals, systems, and projects.

This is where our constant focus is from day to day. Keeping teams flowing inside of the guard rails in the same direction to reach a certain point in a defined amount of time. I always hear, "We manage systems, not people", which is correct, but it is still people running, or are a part of that system.

Managing helps the successful incorporation of new applications into a team's system. Rolling out a new point of sale system; bringing in a new product line; relaunching a training curriculum to the field team that focuses on core fundamentals. All of these have a detailed set of rules that apply to certain teams and must be completed in a precise time and within a specific budget. Contrary to popular belief, managing is not an evil tool. When done correctly, productivity is flowing in the right direction, at the correct speeds, reducing clogs or congestion that slows down the system's throughput.

The effectiveness of a good manager is supported by their style of engagement to give feedback at the right times. Their ability to create a consistent environment for the team, customers, and brand.

There are many styles of management, but let's look at the top three.

Authoritative Management – a strong directive given style that sets the expectations and consequences upfront by project. Authoritative leaders are very clear on the outcome, direction and path that needs to be taken to completion. Now, I don't know about you, but I don't want that as my manager. Like a *50 Shades of Grey* manager. A feeling like there is a constant cracking of a whip, leaving employees feeling used and empty. But seriously, most would describe this setting as one where creativity is stifled. They can be seen as overbearing, especially to employees that are used to some free reign in how they complete tasks. If a team is going through a long period of struggle or change, this would be the best approach for a fast track to success or completion.

This may not be the best management style for all projects or teams, but when time lines are constrained and top line goals are very specific, this style can bring a team across a finish line when no additional input is needed. This approach is also good for inexperienced teams that may not have been working together for very long. But experienced teams may feel like they are taking a step backwards with this method. Try to avoid an authoritative style when it comes to creative outside the box thinking.

Persuasive Management – rather than telling someone what to do, they ask a series of questions to help guide the decision-making process of a team. This style tends to build trust and makes a team feel valued. This style works great with a more experienced team. And should be avoided with newer ones that lack self-direction. Persuasive management styles should also be avoided if teams need clear boundaries because prior managers had loose standards on company directives.

When managed correctly, the persuasive style can be seen as the hybrid between Laissez-faire and Authoritative. You are guiding the team to a specific outcome, but doing so in a sense with questions that may lead in one direction more so than another. When using this style, be sure to lead with facts, rationale, and logic so that the team can get a clear picture of the approach needed for success.

Laissez-faire (less-say-fair) Management – a very hands-off approach to team management. The Laissez-faire style is said to have originated in France in the late 1700s. There term is defined as "allow to do". This style uses a heavy dose of delegation and leaves a lot of control to the key people on the team, creating more freedom for workflow. Employee engagement scores are typically high in this environment. This style is best used for offsite teams or even teams that have a higher skill-set on items than the manager does.

Like any other style, this one should also be used with extreme caution. When this style is poorly managed, conflicts can arise between employees who feel like they are pulling the weight of projects more than other contributors. If efficiency and high productivity is your number one goal as a manager, stay clear of this style when possible.

No matter the style of management, the key principles are still the same. Keeping teams flowing inside of the guard rails in the same direction to reach a certain point in a defined amount of time.

How many of you can remember a manager from your past or even now, that fits one of these molds and helped shape your style today?

Some of us are like, "Yeah, when I worked for Mrs. Ronda, I always wanted to be just like her."

While others are like, "Billy was a real bleep". Didn't even address him by his last name. "Billy was terrible. That's exactly what I didn't want to be like."

Whether you are motivated by a management style you want to be like, or one you want to steer clear from, it doesn't matter. Positive or negative drives home the same result to shape you to be who you are today.

Now, the Leadership Mindset.

In a Leadership Mindset you're KPIs start with understanding the overarching goals of the company, industry trends, and challenges that lie ahead that others may not see. When coming on board as a leader you are supporting your own orientation by getting to know how decisions are made, how innovation takes place, and who has influence in the company. Delegation takes the form of knowing what projects makes the most sense to start in what order, how it affects the culture, and realize the step change needed for success. Then engagement is built around not only getting to know every department and making regular time to listen to your team's needs, but engaging with direct feedback from your customer base and knowing how the customer likes to engage.

Now, leadership styles are different from management styles, but share some similarities. A leadership approach is used when a group of people are having difficulty seeing a path forward, or the next step, and one must define a clear vision without detailed plans of where they need go. It is setting the direction and making the decision to get there. Painting the picture of what success looks like, without the instruction of every brush stroke. And the best leaders, like Aristotle said, have to be great followers.

An effective leader has influence whether they are in the building or not. They have innovation, act decisively, show enthusiasm, courage, and commitment. They also focus on engagement, not just output. They don't focus on their weakness and then try to make it stronger; they acknowledge their weakness and use their teams' strengths to make up for it.

You may notice, I didn't use the word: passion in the definition of leader traits.

Did you know, the definition for passion is - barely controllable emotion, or suffering. Enthusiasm is more closely related to the emotion most are attempting to describe as a strong feeling for a leader. Enthusiasm is eager enjoyment, interest, or approval. In Greek, it means possessed by God, inspired.

Leadership Styles align closely with Management styles. Let's look at a few of the more popular techniques.

Influential Leadership – this style uses the voice of others over their own. Influential leaders are always seeking ways to create wins by turning problems into opportunities to show off the strength of others, not just themselves. Their depth in knowledge of not only their team, but their teams' families, hobbies, anniversaries and more helps to build long lasting connections with the people around them. Although there is a lot of collaboration and high engagement, their team still looks up to the influential leader and asks for guidance, which in return fuels the employees.

Influential leaders also easily attract top talent from many pools. You can feel the influential leader's presence even when they're on vacation. The best time to use influential leadership is when a culture change is needed in an organization. An Influential leadership style is best avoided when one is new to an organization. Connections and commitments are too new to have long lasting effects resonate when you're not present. Be sure to use this style when you're 100% sure of the buy-in from your entire team.

Strategic Leadership – this is creative problem solving at its best. At times the strategic leader can seem introverted because of the constant analyzing, planning, and execution that their mind loops through. But when they communicate out the plan for success, you can tell the devil is in the details. Strategic leaders are heavily KPI driven and fully aware of risks and ROIs. They are also dedicated to finishing the job/project. They don't just paint the picture and leave the rest for others to complete. They roll up their sleeves and get into the details through the last mile. This style is best used to streamline processes, boost productivity, and promote innovation when the time is needed.

Strategic leadership should be avoided at all cost when environments are unpredictable. Whether it is multiple outside forces that have significant change, inside challenges on multiple fronts, or a combination of both. Strategic leadership should be used cautiously. High risk situations may cause this style to second guess themselves causing more issues than it solves. Tunnel vision from sticking to a plan too rigidly will cause this style to stall in success.

Visionary Leadership – visionary leaders change the world even before it knows it needs to be changed. Steve Jobs. Dr. Martin Luther King. Henry Ford. Nelson Mandela. Mahatma Gandhi. Coco Chanel. Inspirational. Magnetic. Bold. They can envision an entire company's future and rally hundreds and thousands of people to meet that future head on while still building the plane to get them there. Visionary leadership is best used when motivation has been lost by the masses. Or a challenge has come up that is so large that no one can see what that next step could be or should be. Then they paint the picture so vividly that everyone can't believe they didn't see the solution before. It's always been in front of their eyes. The visionary leader just helps them to see it. Visionary leaders don't always finish the goal they set for the team. A disconnection from reality can drive this leader to overshoot the runway on company goals. The caution on Visionary Leadership is constantly riding on the edge of overpromising, then under delivering. That's when a leader who is loved by all, can quickly turn into a Pariah.

Can you recall experiencing one of these leadership styles firsthand?

I'm telling you, it's something amazing to witness.

What's common among these leadership styles is the power of persuasion, to ask one to take the next step even before the floor appears. To hop on the plane for flight while it is still being built. Everyone knows it is what it is but chooses to be a part of the team because they can see the destination even before they get there.

Now, for the Coaching Mindset.

I must admit. This one is one is my favorite.

My youngest son plays sports. He's a 16-year-old sophomore in high school and he's been playing sports since he was 7 years old.

Now, I never played sports in school when I was younger, but I did play hooky. And I was good at it. Pole vaulting fences and squatting behind bushes like a track star. Couldn't catch me even when they tried.

The youth sports world is crazy. But it's a real thing. It's a true industry that stands on its own.

Did you know in AAU basketball you can start playing at the age of 7? Now at the age of 7 you have someone's dad coaching you a few hours a week, playing in tournaments locally. AAU season typically runs from March to June.

Once you get to middle school and begin competing at a scholastic level you then graduate to being coached on basic basketball skills and drills. Team effort. Now, middle school season runs from November to March. But you can still play AAU basketball during the off season. At this point, if your kid plays both, they are consistently being coached 9 of 12 months of the year.

If your kid is good, they take it into high school ball. A whole other level. You have multiple coaches teaching more advanced techniques. The season still runs the same, and many players are still playing AAU during the off season. Getting coached 9 out of 12 months of the year.

For those with that special talent, and want to move up a level, you then have college basketball.

At the college basketball level, you are practicing for 4-9 hours per day, multiple days per week, year-round. There is no more AAU at this level. It's grueling, but it gets the very few ready for the NBA.

Now we get to the NBA. Fandom starts. There are 82 games in a season, from October through April, not counting preseason or playoffs. The players at this point are getting paid 10's of millions of dollars a year. They've been getting coached for three quarters of the year since the age of 7. Yet still, there is a coach on the sideline screaming at the top of their lungs, when to press, when to fall back, who to guard, and in between every single game stop, they're pulling the entire team over, even the ones on the bench to talk through the next play. All of this for a ball and hoop.

But at work some supervisors, managers, leaders say, "My team has been working together for the past two years. I don't need to coach them. We don't even need huddles. They know exactly what to do. I pay them $15 an hour, they better know what to do."

The level of complexities in our business far outweighs a ball in hoop. Our entire industry view of ongoing coaching and team huddles must change.

Now, the Coaching Style is very different from the manager and leader style. One could argue that the manager and leader is the mastery of moving large groups.

Coaching can be seen as the mastery of small groups and one on ones. It's a development process that enables someone to build their capabilities so that they can achieve personal, professional, and organizational goals. Lastly, and most importantly, coaching teaches someone how to think and strategize. How to assess a situation in an ever-changing environment. Allowing your team, the autonomy to take medium risks with the confidence to yield maximum results.

A core step for coaching is asking open ended questions that promote interaction by drawing out ideas and information. Who, what, where, when, why, and how helps to generate these answers. These questions, when formulated right, are known as power questions. They draw out answers that require some critical thinking from the person you are asking. You're looking for questions that can:

Draw out a deep meaning.

Open verbal creativity

Build on to more questions.

Create reflective conversations.

And, has the listener curious about new possibilities.

Always imagine that the one you are coaching is the expert of who they are, and your goal is to draw out the information from them as if they are introducing themselves to someone they've never met before.

Closed questions should not be used if possible. The structure of most closed questions pushes one to choose from a predefined set of answers.

Like 'Yes or No', or 'True or False'. Even a set of multiple-choice answers.

Although most people relate coaching styles to management/leadership styles, there are three different types of coaching styles in general.

Democratic Coaching – this style can be seen in action if you've ever watched Ted Lasso. Ted is an American football coach that was hired to run an English Football club in a southwest region of London called Richmond. The Democratic style gives the team input on strategies and approach with the final decision coming from the coach. If an idea fails, it gives experience to both the team and coach. In this environment, small teams know their ideas will be heard and considered, with support given from everyone once the decision is made.

In a one-on-one setting it gives the ability of the one being coached to increase their confidence in making decisions. This coaching style helps to rebuild leaders that have run into failed attempts at leadership and seek rehabilitation in trusting themselves to make the right choices.

The caution in small teams is the mindfulness of not appearing to show favoritism, which can stifle team growth, and damage a coach's integrity. Democratic coaching is also time consuming when the process is done correctly. If time is of the essence, lean into other methods of coaching to yield the best results.

Autocratic Coaching – autocratic coaching is the opposite of Democratic. Autocratic can also be considered less as a style and seen more as a situational technique versus a long-term practice. To use this style effectively the coach must know their team exceptionally well. Knowing the breaking points and motivations of each individually. It is better if both the breaking point and motivation point are the same for most of the people on the team. That way when hard decisions are made, reactions are universal for the most part.

This rings true with individual coaching as well. The one being coached can be stuck in a non-progressive state out of mere choice. If there is enough trust between the Coach, and one being coached, that toughness in the proper amount can yield higher performance.

By offering structure, you can remove confusion when someone is not clear on expectations. If the path forward is complex and high performance from an individual is needed, the autocratic approach can help them maneuver with eyes forward and not looking down exposing the heights of what one may fall to. Again, the trust factor must be 100% between both parties.

If this approach is sustained for long periods, the trust that's built can quickly deteriorate with the one being coached feeling unappreciated and dive deeper into underperformance. In the right hands where the coach is the most knowledgeable person, the results can push performance further than expected.

Holistic Coaching – the holistic style is the elevation of long-term thinking inside and outside the office or field. It's not just teachings that strengthen companies and organizations, it teaches lifelong lessons to your team that far outlasts any P&L.

It puts the importance of being a person first over the position. The lessons taught in this approach may not be seen or used for months or even years in one's career, but the practices are so intense that the student reacts like it's second nature because it just makes sense in the moment.

This style of coaching helps to connect the mind and body through exercises like mindfulness meditation. I believe we all can agree that higher performance is more easily achieved when individuals have reduced stress and improved focus. The higher-level coach can identify individual internal conflict that may be holding one back from progress and help define their personal perspectives, emotions and desires that link to that conflict so one can understand it and approach it from a place of confidence and curiosity.

Many holistic coaches place a focus on values to help guide decision making and goal setting. When we are aiming at goals because it aligns with what we truly believe in, success is much more attainable, even with unforeseen setbacks and challenges.

Like all other styles of Managing, Leading or Coaching, the holistic approach is not for every situation and should be used surgically. Avoid using this approach with individuals or small groups that are more transactional in nature and do not practice deep connections even within themselves. Lastly, holistic coaching is probably best avoided when large organizational change is on the horizon. Starting and not completing this systematic approach will do more than damage than good if not given enough time investment.

Do you believe that managing is the most effective mindset in a professional setting?

Or, do you believe leadership is?

How about coaching?

No matter which one you choose, you are correct. It just depends on what situation the mindset is being applied to how successful your results will be.

Your goal is to explore, enhance and embrace all three mindsets and find out which one you naturally rely on.

We now know the differences in managing, leading, and coaching. One is the mastery of keeping systems or projects moving in the right direction. One is the mastery of painting a picture of what success looks like even if there is not a system in place getting a group of people advance towards that destination. And, one is the mastery of small groups and one on one's that helps draw out the inner performance of a team or individual by asking the right questions to get the one that's being coached to see the answer that was already within themselves.

We talked through the advantages and disadvantages of all three.

But how do we apply the balance of all three today to be more successful tomorrow?

You first must ask yourself, which one of these three do I tend to lean more towards throughout my day? To help answer this question, start by asking yourself the following questions and writing down your answers. When answering use the, Absolutely True, More True, Less True, Absolutely Not-True, method.

1. I have always known that I would not be fulfilled in my career if I was not involved in a helping profession.
2. When someone discusses a problem or challenge with me, my mind automatically begins looking for that person's current strengths.
3. When someone discusses a problem or challenge with me, I begin to describe what a result would look like and have them define their own steps to get there.
4. When someone discusses a problem or challenge with me, I begin to describe what current systems are already in place to help guide them to a better solution.
5. One of my deepest values is nurturing the human

growth process.

6. One of my deepest values is starting a new quest in life and seeing where the journey takes me.
7. One of my deepest values is maintaining the order of my environment so that my expectations consistently meet my reality.
8. I always make sure my team knows what success looks like for their roles.
9. I always make sure my team knows what success looks like for their personal growth.
10. I always make sure my team knows what success looks like for the company as a whole and I link what their contributions are to make that success happen.
11. Over the years, several people have told me that I have a unique ability to help people achieve their goals at an accelerated rate.
12. Over the years, several people have told me that I have a unique ability to give a clear and concise answer to a unique problem.
13. Over the years, several people have told me that I have a unique ability to complete projects through the end.
14. Do I know what's important to my boss?
15. Do I know what's important to the individuals on my team?
16. Do I know what's important to the industry that we may not be seeing right now?

There isn't a right or wrong answer here. It is merely asking which one do you connect with more, even if you connect with all three angles of the same question. That's what helps you define what mindset you more naturally settle in.

I ask that you walk away today exploring and embracing the mindset you find yourself in most and know the balance of when to use the other mindsets to make your results in your week not just happen, but multiply by adopting the right style in the right situations.

If you would like to learn more Leading with The Right Mindset:

Managing vs. Leading vs. Coaching, visit
www.jasonebrooks.com and book a session for my most
requested keynote today.

The Takeaway

We get married to closely to labels in our industry. Believing
that the title is how we must act or present ourselves during the
entirety of our workday. This one lane thinking will inevitably
lead us down the wrong road at dangerous speeds until it is too
late. Before we try to decipher what a manager, leader, or
coach would do, we first must decide what is the best result for
a situation. Both short term and long term.

Although more companies have invested in management and
leadership development, a larger piece of the puzzle that's
missing is coaching. This may be because professional
coaching is viewed as something reserved for the top 1% of
professionals. But when coaching investments are measured, it
far out scales the returns of management and leadership
development.

Because of this the differences, advantages, & disadvantages
of managing, leading and coaching mindset needs to be
understood. And not just understood, but taught and available
at all levels in every company. Your mindset influences how you
think, feel, and react in your professional and personal
environment. The mindset that you're in any given situation will
either strengthen or weaken your ability to succeed.

Whether managing your team to higher productivity, or painting
a picture to what the next step is to advance the brand. Or even
mastering your one on one's to exceed individual and
organizational goals. It's all about getting into the correct
vehicle that yields the best results and creating a win-win in the
time frame that allows it. Just don't get stuck in one mindset for
multiple situations. Know what your natural tendency leans
towards, be polished enough to execute the other mindsets,
and lean on your team to help fill the gaps that you're not strong

at. Just be sure to have all three mindsets at your disposal to use to increase your success.

The Angle

Managing – ensuring the vision is executed. Leading – ensuring the vision is communicated. Coaching – ensuring the team received constant feedback on performance.

*   **-Kimberly Grant** *– Fortune 100 Director, Performance Food Group, Washington DC*

In my opinion they are all closely related. Managing is executing a process, SOP, recipe, guideline that's been established by the company. A manager isn't always focusing on managing people but the process. Managing labor, food cost, beverage cost, plate cost, etc…

Leading is not only leading by example but leading through situational experience. Teaching and helping people to grow in their positions and understand what it takes to get to the next level. "I've been in that situation before and this is how I handled it".

Coaching is more directed towards personal development. "Can I give you some advice on how I would've handled that situation differently than you did"? "I was listening to the way you were speaking to that team member and if it were me this is how I would've handled it". You can never those words, always speak in a calm and forgiving voice, never curse, never yell, etc… Then circle back and check in with them to make sure you were understood and can you clarify anything else after it's processed.

*   **-Mike Moore** *– COO, Yardbird Group, Miami FL*

Managing is pure transaction, moving pieces from one place to another. It's very time consuming because generally the pieces don't move unless you're there to move them, or they move to places you don't want them to go.

Leading is about creating the image that you are someone people should want to follow. It's crafting the perception of how people see you. It's easily (and often) faked, but if you, your company, or your idea is not really worth following the trust you're given doesn't last long. It turns into animosity because people feel "fooled", that can quickly lead to a toxic culture. Conversely if you live the values you speak of, they will follow you anywhere.

Coaching is about crafting the perception of how people see themselves. It's starts with convincing them they should do a certain thing, then that they can do that thing, then showing them how and letting them fail safely until they can nail it, time and again.

Pick 2 - I've rarely met someone who was truly proficient in all 3. As soon as I do, I'll be following them.

    -Pat Peterson *- Senior VP of Restaurants, Wagamama USA, NY NY*

In simplest terms, Managing = Doing; Leading = Inspiring; and Coaching = Helping. To be a highly effective leader or team member, I think you have to be skilled at and willing to do all 3 at different times. Knowing when each is required and how best to do it is the art.

    -Coley O'Brien *– Chief People Officer, The Wendy's Company, Dublin OH*

On a Side Note:

Write Down and Follow Up On Everything

Your brain is a steel trap, and anything that crosses it is caught, and never escapes.

When's the last time you said that with a straight face?

The tasks, duties, responsibilities, and accountability of a hospitality leader is wide and deep like the Pacific Ocean. With that comes a vast arena of questions, comments, and concerns from multiple people on your team. As they look to you for guidance, your attention to detail and timeliness should be prevalent when it comes to passing on information, directions and answering questions. The best way to help you live up to that expectation is note taking.

Call me an old-school fool, but I've never been impressed with exhibitions of a young, sponge-like mind from a server that never writes down an order. Their intense gaze of a street corner magician never fazes me. As a matter of fact, I find myself looking for the smallest mistakes that are made that can be blamed on not writing the specifics of my families order or questions on a menu item. I can almost assure that you do the same as well.

Then when I see someone rapidly scribing the finer details of our likings and there is still a mistake, I find myself blaming the kitchen or the POS, only because I feel that my server did everything in their power to get it right, simply because they wrote it down.

Your team looks at you the same way. The visual of you writing down a question or comment that they made makes them feel for lack of better terms, special, because you are finding what they are saying is important enough to remember and jot down. This goes a long way in relationship building with your team. It will also help you to clarify the specifics of what they are asking to make sure you are researching the right information for them.

Getting it right the first time adds to the success of you building your credibility as a leader.

Now for the follow up. You do not want to be known as a dog with no teeth, someone who flies by night, the next flavor of the month, the leader who avoids confrontation, or spineless and lazy.

Depending on the type of follow up, you can be viewed as any of the above for not following up on a direct order you've given, a question from a subordinate, or task at hand. In standing out above your peers and building a lasting impression in your organization, the timely follow up from a note that was written down is everything.

I always keep two notebooks in my travel bag. One for personal notes and one for business, and I always carry the work one with me when on-site. A lot of leaders now use note taking apps like Evernote, OneNote, Notebook, or SuperNote to jot down information and sync to multiple devices. Digital notes also bring peace of mind in case a notebook is misplaced or damaged. One of the downsides to digital note taking is that it can appear that you're banging out a quick text message or email versus listening to someone's concerns. It can be misinterpreted and sends the wrong message at times. Try to stick to pen and pad whenever possible.

Last is scheduling yourself a routine of reflecting on your notes twice daily. We tend to find ourselves struggling during the waking morning to remember an important task you know you had for that afternoon, but just can't recall. Some of these are personal tasks, some professional. Then the day ends and like magic you remember hours after the time we wanted it complete. My go-to times for note reflection are between 7:00-9:30am, 1:00-2:30pm, and 4:00-5:00pm. You only need 5-10 minutes to go back over them. But you'll find yourself shaving wasted hours off your day by getting the more important items completed and following up on items for your team to help them be successful.

Whichever your style of note taking I urge you to take the time to do so and follow up on your notes at the beginning, mid-day and end of day daily. Again, timeliness is everything and making sure you get back to your team on time says a lot in your dedication to make sure they have the right answers to make the right decisions.

Master Your Meetings

The Main Course

Mastering successful meetings in the hospitality industry is a challenge. The whole premise of what we do is based on actionable items through tight deadlines that deal with multiple human interactions in a fast-paced environment. With that in mind, the same principles and importance can be emphasized for multiple industries, not just in hospitality. The following tips may then be for life, not just the restaurant.

Taking the time to pull oneself out of the fray and sit down at a table to discuss numbers and strategy can seem like a bore. In most veteran minds, the need to attend a meeting is like the need to watch water boil. Most would rather be doing something else.

I, however, believe in the contrary. Having meetings is a necessity; it's just that we are rarely taught how to Master them to make the invested time and strategy worth it for all parties involved.

The reason why we tend to view meetings as a waste is because, first: it's hard to stay focused when sitting at a table for multiple hours. Second: it's rare for someone to state what the main objective of the meeting is without the meeting being hijacked by other topics. Lastly: everyone attending always feels unproductive when a decision is not reached on the main objective and a meeting ends in the same state in which it started. This is the reason why most employees feel that meetings are not necessary and a waste of time.

As promised, this book is based as a short read on important topics that managers can act on immediately and grow their leadership skills in the eyes of their team and their boss, so let's get right into it.

According to Oxford Dictionary, a meeting is – '*An assembly of people for a particular purpose, especially for formal discussion.*' Meeting. (n.d.). In Oxford English dictionary. Retrieved from https://www.lexico.com/en/definition/meeting

Although the outcome of some meetings can be mildly formal, the reason we should arrange for a meeting is not just to have a discussion, but to reach a necessary outcome that would not have been reached without the assembly of specific individuals. Meaning, the outcome that was reached when everyone gets up from the table moves the needle further to success, and most of the attendees feel the same way. At all costs, you should refrain from having a meeting just to have one.

Meetings can also be scheduled to make sure that all parties are kept updated on current events that directly involve their area of responsibility and to share ideas and best practices with like individuals for professional development.

This leads us to the very first tip for mastering your meetings – have an agenda.

Your agenda should be created in a thoughtful manner that covers relevant content for those who attend and stays on track 100% of the time. Know this, the agenda will always make or break your attempt to wrangle in multiple personalities to focus on the same thing at the same time and have all attendees contribute confidently. At this point, you probably know the topics you want to cover, but how do you make sure that it is successful in the sense that you met the objective of having everyone attend? Part of that success is knowing what you want out of the meeting and defining that clearly in the agenda. The approach for an agenda with reoccurring meetings versus one-off meetings should be dealt with differently.

For example, if you have reoccurring bi-weekly meetings with your assistant managers and shift leaders, as the GM, you can state that your objective of the meeting is to have all departments report on the development of their top 3 and bottom 3 people, review unforeseen changes on KPIs in their areas of responsibilities, and update other departments on ongoing projects that affect everyone.

Whatever the objective for scheduling a meeting, the first rule is to clearly state the objective and make sure your agenda matches it. You also must state what kind of participation you expect from the attendees. Whether they will be presenting during certain topics, or if it will be a 90% data dump with just a few minutes for Q&A. Having your team prepared as much in advance as possible is key.

To keep your meeting relevant to your topics and listed agenda, I suggest something as simple as printing out your agenda and reviewing it at the start of every meeting. Many of us have multiple things going on in our heads every waking moment. Just because you announced two days ago what the meeting was pertaining to, doesn't mean your team remembers what will be discussed. Typing up the agenda and having a printed format, or even a slide in your deck (PPT Presentation) for them to review, always gives them a reminder of what they should be prepared for. You can take it a step further and have the agenda sent to all attendees 48 hours prior to the meeting. Be cautious that you may have to prework your attendees before sending out the agenda if there are sensitive topics that you may get pushback on. We will cover prework a little later in this chapter.

Most people do not like having surprise content in meetings. Ideally, it is best to inform everyone who needs to attend the meeting 48 hours in advance of what will be discussed if it is a reoccurring meeting. If not, then at least having an agenda to review at the start of the meeting is needed. If this is a one-off meeting, plan to get the information out 5-7 days in advance to give attendees time for schedules to be changed and gather what information they feel they need to bring.

When building out agendas for reoccurring meetings, your agenda should be cookie-cutter in structure to help your team become familiar with the process. The upcoming illustration shows an agenda that has a meeting being led by a Multi-Unit Manager with General Managers in attendance. The meeting's agenda has three main sections. WIGs, The Whirlwind, and Open Discussion.

The structure of the agenda can be traced back to the FranklinCovey Institutes book 'The 4 Disciplines of Execution' by Chris McChesney, Sean Covey & Jim Huling.

The principle of 'The 4 Disciplines of Execution', or 4DX, is to focus on four things to help bring about the success that you, as the leader, clearly define.

1. Focus on the Wildly Important Goals (WIGs)

2. Act on Lead Measures

3. Keep a Compelling Scoreboard

4. Create a Cadence of Accountability

None of these are new processes in the Leadership world. They are however spelled out clearly and help give guidance to attain success in reaching your Wildly Important Goals.

This agenda has 4 main topics (WIGs) that are always covered in every meeting because they feel that this is what their success will be measured by, and an additional 2-3 changing topics (the Whirlwind) that just drives you crazy week to week but are still of importance. The Whirlwind can be defined as things that are far removed from your main goals, and you can't stand dealing with them, but are still necessary for you to run a successful business.

This example shows that their main goals (WIG') involve:

Sales & P&Ls

Guest Satisfaction Surveys

Food Safety Inspections and Audits

Team Development / Training / Hiring

Agenda
P3 Week 4

<u>(15 Minutes)</u>   **Sales & P&L Review**
- Sales - WTD, PTD, YTD, Declining Budgets, P&L's, COGS

<u>(5 Minutes)</u>   **Guest Satisfaction Survey Review**
- Last Week & QTD

<u>(15 Minutes)</u>   **Food Safety Standards**
- Most Current Inspections & Audits

<u>(20 Minutes)</u>   **Team Development Review**
- Staffing Pars/Training/Hiring Updates

<u>(10 Minutes)</u>   **Mid-Year Evals**

<u>(5 Minutes)</u>   **Employee Injury Protocol**

<u>(10 Minutes)</u>   **Payroll Procedure Changes**

<u>(5 Minutes)</u>   **Upcoming Marketing Events & Promotions**

<u>(5 Minutes)</u>   **Wrap Up / Open Discussion**

Their top 4 will be structured the exact same way each week and will always be reviewed with the most up to date sales, scores and discussions. To master this portion, it will be best to know how much you want to speak and how much interaction you are expecting from your team. I suggest making sure when your present/host your meeting at least half of your comments end with a question mark. When you're switching from page to page or slide to slide, begin the next section with something like,

'How many of you hit your sales goals for the week?'

Or

'Who thinks they had the best Guest Service scores last week?'

Or

'How many of you know exactly what happened with your Food Cost last week?'

This gives the opportunity to break from a data-dump from Mr. Know-It-All, and gives the attendees a chance to chime in at the beginning of the topic, versus the end when you've already told them what to think. The more frequently your team can raise their hands in agreeance, or answer questions throughout a meeting, the more it gives their brains the opportunity to reset from the constant listening of one voice.

In the figure above, you will also see that each topic has an allotted time frame for discussion. It is not an exact science, but as you use the time stamp you will notice that attendees will help to reel in extended discussions that may be unnecessary to make sure that all topics are reached during the meeting.

The next tip to mastering your meetings – the content being delivered should designate who needs to be invited to the meeting. The people that are invited to the meetings are the ones that are key decision makers in that department. Some may argue that influential people should also be invited to the meeting. Your key person of influence could be a team member with 10 years of tenure that multiple people lean on for her insight. That does not mean that they should be at the table with department heads that make decisions. The influencer will be needed to implement new strategies and get other people on board quickly. Not when making decisions. When you invite associates and/or departments for representation that do not have deliverables on the content, you open the door for hijacking of time and discussions on content that has nothing to do with the original meeting agenda.

You also must ensure that those invited to the meeting have their schedules cleared for the time frame for them to attend. Now remember, we are dealing with the hospitality industry, not a software tech office where we are coordinating flights, hotel rooms, and time zones in Western Europe to make sure all parties are able to attend. You still must keep in mind schedules and coverage as you pull people out of place for 30-90 minutes.

Next, when considering invitees, you should also list what the attendees will be in charge of during the meeting and what they will be reporting out on. For example, you will need someone in charge of timekeeping. Making sure too much time is not spent on certain sections. Your agenda should have time allotments beside each section to help everyone have an understanding that they must get to the core of that section quickly, without bringing up topics that need to be sidelined. Your timekeeper will be allowed to have a digital clock or stopwatch at the table to insure you do not go over time on certain topics. I do not suggest a cell phone or tablet as notifications may disturb the timekeeper.

You will also need a minute-taker, recording key information, decisions, and unanswered questions during the meeting so you can send out notes or minutes after the meeting as a digital hard copy of what was covered.

If a person's only goal is to listen during the entire meeting and not contribute with predetermined content, I would argue that they are not needed at the meeting to begin with.

If you find that some topics bring up multiple opinions, push back or questions that means either:

1. You did not do enough pre-work around that topic prior to the meeting to insure everyone was on the same page on a way forward.
2. You did not allot enough time for this topic, and it could be so important that it needs to be addressed in a separate meeting by itself.
3. There may be multiple people at the meeting who

are not decision-makers on that topic, and a separate meeting is needed for only those who need to be there to get to a decision correctly and quickly with the right pre-work.

Pre-work can be defined two different ways.

1. Work that needs to be completed by attendees before attending a meeting that can be viewed as a 'sneak peek' into what will be discussed and gives attendees a leg up on giving answers or providing information. Examples are questionnaires, research on specific content, and information about the attendee's background so that the presenter gets to know the room better.

2. Probing attendees prior to a meeting about certain important information that will be discussed at a meeting and answering questions or concerns to help ensure the presenter knows what the reaction will be and refrain from excessive time being spent on the subject.

We're using the second definition of pre-work for our examples. If you're looking to introduce a major change to how schedules are written, or how and when tip out is allocated, you most likely want to know how your team is going to react to something before glazing over it at a meeting. Something that you think should take 10 minutes can last 30 minutes because you underestimated their reactions. Pre-work is a detrimental tool to any leader's war chest especially when dealing with major change for your organization and getting your team on the same page quickly in one room.

One of the secrets to being a Master of Meetings is outlining ground rules for your meetings to your team. Setting the stage for this is letting all attendees know that you will always start on time, every time. As well as end on time and not go over what you asked your attendees to set aside for their day. If your meeting is set for 1:00 pm and only 7 of 12 attendees are there, you start the meeting at exactly 1:00 pm. This does a few things. It shows the attendees who took time to make sure they were there early and on time that you value their punctuality, and it teaches those who run behind that the meeting will start regardless of whether they are there or not. This flight will not sit idling for late passengers.

Do not restart the meeting or topics once latecomers arrive. Have them depend on someone else to fill them in later. Time is respect in every industry, not just hospitality. That goes for our guests and our teams.

Going back to the beginning of this chapter, the reason you called for a meeting was because there were decisions that needed to be made that would not have had the opportunity to be made unless they were discussed with all who attended the meeting. This means that these decisions should only be made at the meeting table and not post-meeting. There is nothing more confusing than telling your team that they are the leaders that help make things happen, ask them their opinion on a major change, then tell them you will give them a final decision on a later date. If this is so, then why ask their opinion in the first place? Decisions must be made at the table with your team in attendance if you are asking for their feedback. If you do not follow that, this act alone will underscore the fact that attending meetings is detrimental to your team's success.

Lastly, even with juggling who to attend, when to let them know, what is being covered, the amount of interaction, and layering in structure to ensure success… you need to take notes during the meeting. Some of the best leaders in any industry follow up on everything (see: On A Side Note – Write Down and Follow Up on Everything), and the key to that is note taking.

If you are only able to give great info in bite size pieces but are unable to receive information and questions as well as follow up on it, then you have already closed half of the information highway. The best way to do this is to assign a recorder that will record all follow up conversations, questions, and concerns. For those that arrived at the meeting late, they can reach out to the recorder of the meeting for necessary notes. Although many professionals say you should not have any electronics in a meeting, I've experienced it is best to have the minute-taker typing up notes during the meeting that can immediately be disseminated after the meeting for follow up. It also makes it easier to hand out meeting notes to attendees instead of having to transcribe someone's handwritten notes first. Don't be afraid to rotate this role. Most people will take their own notes during meetings, and for those that don't, this helps to embed the habit of taking notes to make sure they have takeaway content after the wrap up.

The Takeaway

At times it feels that Hospitality Leaders are not built to be Masters of Meetings. This thought needs to be 86'd immediately. Meetings in our world make all the difference in the successful execution of major changes and having a team of 20 focusing on the wrong 20 things at the same time. You must clearly define if you need one and when. A meeting is only held if decisions cannot be made, and information cannot be shared if the ones who attend are not there. Define who should be in attendance, which are only the decision makers. The influencers can be brought on board only after the decisions are made.

Pre-work the attendees by having direct conversations about content that may be sensitive and see what their thoughts are on the topic or change. Refrain from having surprise reactions that derail everyone's time and decision-making abilities during the meeting.

Type up your agenda and add time allotments by each topic and stick to it. Time is precious to all in attendance, especially when we deal with such tight labor budgets. If the meeting is reoccurring, have 3-4 main topics that are always discussed that cover your Wildly Important Goals and a section for Whirlwind items to be discussed. Don't data dump, find ways at the beginning of each new topic to get the attendees to answer a question or raise their hands in a motion of votes to get blood circulating and brain waves to reset.

Start and end on time every time, no matter who is running late. Again, time is precious to everyone in the room, and you should reward those who made the effort to be early and on time.

Know your objective and make decisions only at the meeting table. Don't side-table a decision because you want to think about it. If that's the case, then why ask everyone to rearrange their day to attend in the first place?

Finally, take notes by assigning someone the task of writing down pertinent questions that need more research or sidebar topics that may have been raised during the open discussion portion. Follow up on everything. If we say it, then do it. Accountability, or the lack of spreads quickly, and you want to make sure you are spreading the positive aspect of accountability.

The Angle

First, I always start meeting with an agenda that includes an objective; why are we meeting and what are we trying to accomplish. Next, if the meeting is a staff meeting to include department updates, I kick the meeting off with "weekly wins", where everyone chimes in with accomplishments for the last week, progress on key initiatives and even personal wins. The purpose of the weekly wins is multi-faceted, including getting the meeting started on a positive note, getting everyone to contribute, sharing appreciation for each other and general positivity. All these things help to build relationships and lead to collaboration on challenges that may arise in the remainder of the meeting. Finally, after the meeting, I think it's critical to send a recap with key decisions made and follow up items, including key owners and timing.

-Paul Macaluso – *President & CEO, Another Broken Egg, Orlando FL*

Generally, I set the stage at the beginning of the meeting. I establish the needs/wants of the meeting and what I consider very important – the why. Without understanding the "why" we are meeting the dialogue often gets distracted and off course. "Why" gives a purpose to the meeting and feels less like a dissertation and more of a joint purpose.

*-**Sean Keyes** – VP Design & Construction, Focus Brands, Lancaster PA*

Always go into a meeting with a desired outcome, whether it is setting the stage for a future decision, building a key relationship, gaining a deeper learning or getting to a specific decision/outcome. If you state the objective up front (even prior to the meeting), then the group will be a lot closer to meeting the objectives. Additionally, a quick recap at the end making sure that everyone has their marching orders on what they are responsible for next.

*-**Alan Magee** – VP Marketing & Communications, Empire Portfolio Group, NY NY*

First is time. Meetings should be scheduled in 15-minute increments (vs. auto default for 1 hour). Second is content. All meetings should have an agenda which is shared in advance. One person should be responsible for taking notes and distributing after meeting ends.

*-**Kimberly Grant** – Fortune 100 Director, Performance Food Group, Washington DC*

When I think about the best meetings I've been a part of, I walk away feeling like progress has clearly been made, collaboration and alignment has been achieved, time has been well spent and resources have been well utilized. I've felt equally that way about 8-hour meetings and 15-minute meetings. Mastering meeting facilitation is both art and science, but at a minimum I think it requires having a clear and meaningful purpose, having a clear agenda, ensuring the right people are involved and engaged, ensuring all voices are heard and being respectful of people's time.

*-**Coley O'Brien** - Chief People Officer, The Wendy's Company, Dublin OH*

Never. Stop. Training.

The Main Course

At times it seems that we are the masters of our own demise. Creating unbreakable rules, schedules and templates that should be followed to the 'T' and no further. And the 'T' I am referring to is (T)raining Schedules and (T)emplates. I am a firm believer that too much rigidity in any process causes our team and structure to break instead of strengthening it. Flexibility with form is the first key to success through proper training. The next key must be to never. Stop. Training.

When any acquaintance of ours outside the hospitality industry talks about their day that starts at 9:00 am and ends at 5:00 pm Monday through Friday, we find a way to spew off about how complex the hospitality industry is and the numerous variables we deal with while training talent that is typically fresh out of high school.

They then continue on about their meticulous data entry tasks, coffee break pranks, and water cooler gossip. They also mention how they go on quarterly training exercises with team Olympics, overnight camping, scavenger hunts, mystery dinners, and escape rooms. These are with associates and employees who went to college for 4 years to get their foot in account management and coding. Our jealousy kicks in…

I refuse to believe it is because we, hospitalitarians, do not value training as much as Wall Street or Silicon Valley. We just make smaller budgets.

Notice, I say make, not have.

On average, a restaurant spends about 5% of its total sales on marketing annually. For training, they train a new employee for 2-3 weeks, about 80 hours, or just under 1% of an annual budget. With a new employee hourly rate of $12 per hour, that is $960. If we hired 1 employee per month, every month of the year, that's just under $12,000 spent annually. The marketing budget for a $1 million restaurant at 5% is $50,000. Now, I love my marketing team and they work hard at what they do. I also find it hard to believe that something that is hard to track, like marketing ROI on some campaigns, yields us a better return than proper training at the tune of 5-to-1 if we compare it to building sales.

No one is saying to slash the budget on digital ads and geotargeting, but we must find a balance on the importance of increasing our training budgets that doesn't take away from profitability. The importance of training and finding ways to stretch it from a 2-week training program to a system and mentality that is ongoing to build the best team surrounding us to help run our business is the end that justifies the means.

The question is how.

How do we do transform a shoestring budget into a training ecosystem that lives and breathes in an ever-changing industry?

In the previous chapters, we have graphs, diagrams, and visual aids that can help one get started with modifying their own style with an actionable item. This is much harder with training because every concept, industry, and even individual is different. From the environment to the personality and learning style, there are a million variables that decrease the possibility of a cookie-cutter starting point for all.

The first step we can take is ensuring that training starts with the whole building on day one. From curb to back door. We currently inadvertently train new hires on day one to only own their position, then expect, hopefully, one day, they branch out to want responsibility in more. This happens when we complete orientation at a table with uniforms and paperwork, then walk them back to complete some computer-based training for a few hours, then finally introduce them to their first position/role. This is wrong. When you think about it, we are subconsciously teaching them that when they walk in the door for the next few weeks or even months, the only thing that they should be concerned with is a computer screen and that position.

A better approach is to give a tour of your business through the guest's eyes, starting from the curb. Remember, this is how your customers view your business. They see it from the road, in a vehicle as they are passing by, and they view the whole thing. Walk them around the exterior, pointing out what they may or may not see that usually adds to the guest experience, or that takes away from it. When the exterior is complete, enter the doors and talk through the sight lines of what every customer sees as they walk in. Is it trash cans? Clutter? Open Spaces? Team Members? As you walk them through, describe what a 1-, 3-, or 5-star service is for that area, view, or even interaction, with 1 being the lowest and 5 the highest.

As you're doing this a few things begin to click for your new addition to your team. They now look at the building much differently knowing that they can have an impact on the business from when they pull up, not just when in position. When they are in guest areas, not just in their immediate position. They also get a numerical understanding of what sub-par, par, and above-par service and/or cleanliness is. All on the first day of orientation. Depending on the size and layout of your business, this will add an additional 15-25 minutes to your usual orientation but will give you and your team a return that lasts their entire time under your leadership.

Next, be honest with them about the current status of their colleagues' training, and the expectation of their training as they move through their program. This is a difficult ask. As leaders, we like to paint a picture of our grass being the greenest anyone has ever seen, and we know we can sometimes struggle to keep up with expectations from our direct supervisor as well as compete with our own colleagues in sister stores. Nothing stings harder than the disappointment that we create through false expectations for a new hire. Be truthful to the fact that this new hire may be further in the knowledge of specs and processes in the next 4 months than some of your current employees. This will give the new hire something to strive for, versus feeling misled and confused when others are not completing tasks to standards that they have been trained to.

On the other end of the spectrum, your location may be different. You may have certified trainers in every position in your building that hold the standard on Tell, Show, Do, Review. This is Awesome. The conversation with your new hire is then based on the high expectations throughout the process and the feedback wanted on their experience as they are onboarded, trained, acclimated, and finally transitioned into a solid contributor on the team. Either way, the goal is to be honest with their journey upfront so that their path is easier to follow.

Besides having training programs designed for specific positions that encompass a complete onboarding experience, your training program should always align with your business goals. This means that annually, you will be revamping, if not the least tweaking, your training program according to the most important goals that are rolled out and/or updated by your company. Easier said than done? Absolutely. But the title of this chapter isn't 'Make Training Easier,' it's 'Never Stop Training.' Heck, we could even give it a subtitle of, 'Aways Make Your Training Better', and it would be relevant.

In chapter 1, we covered knowing your KPIs and the

importance of them. That approach sets your team up for knowing what to focus on throughout the week and month. When you purposefully align your training structure with your business goals, the progress from day 1 with new hires as the positive momentum swings towards exceeding those goals is exponentially successful. Now, add in the cross-training of current team members and your business results will be endless.

I do not believe that you should be rewriting the entire company training program annually. You should, however, incorporate the content of newly formed goals and/or technology into the ongoing training of your team as periodically as possible.

For example, if the company goals are to increase Secret Shopper scores to 85% or better by year-end, increase Guest Survey scores to 85% or better by year-end, and increase Health Inspection scores to 95% or better, your team will not get there with an average training schedule for a key position in your business.

A separate training system that incorporates what is on a Secret Shopper score, how the questions are weighted, and what a perfect score looks like, needs to be trained into all team members that interact with customers during their visit. This goes back to the 1-, 3-, & 5-star explanation of key positions referenced earlier.

For Guest Survey scores that are ranked 1-5 your team needs to know what a 1 on service looks like, what a 3 on service is (average), and what a 5 on that survey is by position. This aspect would best be introduced during orientation, setting the stage for the new hire of the expectations from day 1.

For Health Inspections, a great example of ongoing training and aligning it with company goals is printing out an inspection form with all items covered and having a key team member walk through and complete it Bi-weekly, then review the findings with you. The expectation should not be that the team member knows how to approach and answer each item on the inspection. The goal is for them to become more familiar with the content covered and ask questions for clarification on items that may need attention.

As you're going through the exercise of how to align your training with your company goals you may find that orientation is the perfect opportunity for employees to get level-set on culture and standards while understanding the position expectations. In this, you will also realize that you have current team members who went through a poor orientation in the past. I suggest inviting current team members to sit through a new hire orientation until all current team members have been reintroduced to the culture and expectations.

In the end, your goal is to keep your team relevant to your brand by periodically redefining positions, content, and processes in our ever-changing industry.

As a solid rule of thumb, new hire training starts during the interview process and never ends. To be blunt, the best trainers no matter what their actual title is, start brainwashing all candidates well before they are hired by purposefully staging the interview process, questions, and expectations around lifelong training. This can be considered as the foundation in transforming your training program.

These days, the average hospitality interview starts with celebrating the fact that someone made it to the interview because 8 of the last 10 candidates you contacted never showed up. Seriously. The excitement you have is almost so overbearing, that the candidate swears they hear you say, "Yes, you're hired", on the way to the table.

Hide your elation, you must. – 'Yoda'

Honestly, it's not complicated, and it has to be more than just slapped together. Making the time and enduring the patience are the two largest obstacles to having a solid start to your system. It is also not a one-woman show. Your team of leaders must be on the same page as you, which is where a lot of teams get lost in the details of *how* to train. Consistency, relevance of the role and goals, and training continuance through one's entire tenure in your building is great but having a team of people making sure this is well executed puts success in arms reach.

It's also not about perfection. You cannot and will not create aces out of every new addition to your team. You will, however, make them better than when they first joined your team. The average new contributor you're hiring is a 3 of 5. In most examples, we are no longer screening for 4s or better. This means our ability to train talent to increase their productivity in a short amount of time must be more focused and intentional. Our level of execution in this must be on a level of mastery through coaching, influence, and development. Use your company's internal resources to help you and your team make this a reality. As you stumble, make mistakes, and create setbacks at times, know that it is a part of the process. Just be clear about your intentions for your team, get them on the same page, and make the process about the whole experience from interview to departure.

Lastly, and probably the most controversial point, is that training even continues when an employee exits your team. Training should include teaching them how to transition out of their role, update their immediate team on their progress YTD that is aligned with company goals, and steps to take as they join their new company. Think about that last part. We want to help them on how to best enter their next line of work, which has a high probability of being one of our competitors, so that they can achieve success at a higher rate. Most leaders want to cut their losses as quickly as possible when a notice is given in order to give attention to an upcoming candidate for that position. That is nonsense. Having a staff of 25 that shifts to 26 does not give you less time. Meaning, still focusing on training the 25th team member that has 2 weeks left while adding on the 26th new hire does not dilute your time or effort. The same can be said for 30 to 31, or 50 to 51.

As you assist your outward transitioning team members, they are reminded of the investment you have given them from day one up to this day. Talking them through the best approach with a new direct supervisor, shifting into a new hire training mindset, and how to join a new business family. This does a few things. We know that the grass is not always greener on the other side. A poor onboarding experience by their future employer may spark feelings of wanting to rejoin your team. New hires also always speak with their new teams about their old companies. Someone on that team may be considering making a move and hearing the experience of the assistance given during their offboarding can spark them to make the move to your team. Lastly, your reputation, as seen in the eyes of the rest of your team, is solidified even more as they see you as a true mentor, professional, and leader in your industry. After all, as I said, every leader *needs* followers. This is a great way of making one for life.

The Takeaway

Navigating the realm of excellent ongoing and effective training is tricky. Flexibility in what is thought to be a ridged process helps keep your training program forward-thinking and relevant in today's ever-changing industry. If you have the power to change it, make your training budget more realistic with the ROI you will receive from having throughput increase faster from your new hires. If you do not have the power to change it, then make sure you are prioritizing your training practices with your company goals and KPIs to ensure your location is meeting the brand expectations year to year.

Do not inadvertently train your team to have ownership of a single station or position when they first onboard and complete orientation. Incorporate whole building ownership into the first day with a tour of the exterior, interior, and customer interaction areas, as well as their position so that they understand how it all connects. During the tour, give numerical comparisons of standard, above standard, and below standard interactions and execution.

The goal is to always make your training better, not just never stop training. This is possible by reviewing your training annually or as initiatives change at the store level, not just at the company level.

Finally, start the training mindset during the interview process by holding expectations and being truthful about your team. Keep the expectations real and deliver on them. Then, train all the way through until their last day, even if they put in a notice, and then train them on how to transition into a new company, as well as have them update you and your team on their current projects, successes, or challenges. Your goal is to leave them better than when you found them.

The amount of time, energy, and resources given to try not to have turnover in the first 6 months of a new hire, or even in less than 90 days, is a very high ask in our industry. But with practice and focus comes mastery and results in creating an environment that that keeps your team learning, remain above the standard, and stay relevant in the unforeseeable future.

The Angle

The staff that touches the guests are by far our most treasured asset. To be effective and successful, they must be challenged and constantly learning. They get bored so easily. The secret is to have a continuous program/workshop/time for learning set up on a cadence calendar. We conduct tastings of new items, tastings of core items, wine workshops that are hands on and have a story to tell, a new service technique, a new cocktail, etc…

If you're worried about your labor, make it voluntary and you'll see who truly cares. Those are the people you want to invest in.

*-**Mike Moore** – COO, Yardbird Group, Miami FL*

Implementing and maintaining a culture of learning requires consistency and motivation to meeting your long terms goals. Often times, managers lose focus on coaching and training their teams because they are busy with tasks. Overcoming this takes a constant drive to look forward at what the team could become.

-Julie Thompson – *Senior Instructional Design, Zaxby's Grill, Atlanta GA*

Anyone who stops learning is old, whether at twenty or eighty. Anyone who keeps learning stays young.

-Henry Ford – *Founder, Ford Motor Company, Detroit MI*

Training is everything. The peach was once a bitter almond; cauliflower is nothing but cabbage with a college education.

-Mark Twain – *Writer/Entrepreneur, Redding, CT*

I fear not the man who has practiced 10,000 kicks once, but I fear the man who has practiced one kick 10,000 times.

-Bruce Lee – *Martial Arts Master/Actor, Kowloon Tong Hong Kong*

Right now, your competition is training.

-Unknown

On a Side Note:

Accept Accountability for Everything

One of the most challenging things to do as a leader is to accept responsibility for anything that happens in your restaurant. Whether on shift, on vacation or even outside of the country. It's easy to blame an incompetent manager for the firestorm shift or missed truck order. It's even harder to give 100% of the credit to a shift leader who got things right under your guidance.

But this is one of the things that the greats do. A great example can be seen in Key #3 – Delegate by Creating Mini-GMs.

The reason why this side note is so important is because whether you are looked up to by all on your team, or despised by the same number, your team at some point will mock your approach to challenges and successes, and sometimes unknowingly.

Even after weeks of training and following up to get things right, if a mistake is made on a development technique with new hires, the responsibility is still yours. If food cost finally falls in line after 6 months of focus and making it a priority without shorting integrity, the credit goes to the team that was overseeing it, not yourself. Most people find it very frustratingly difficult to balance both ends of this spectrum day to day without pointing fingers when it feels convenient.

One way to start this process of accountability for yourself when goals are not met is to understand your own expectations, then master how you communicate those expectations out to your team in tone, consistency, frequency, and clarity.

You must also be proactive instead of reactive by always evaluating how effective your efforts are in the workplace. Create solutions when you see challenges begin to stir, don't wait until it becomes a bigger problem. Accept criticism from all levels and be open to giving and receiving feedback. Instead of taking the feedback personally, know these are angles that will

Jason E. Brooks

help you grow. When you disagree with others on a process or approach, do so maturely. We don't always agree with everyone on a solution, but we must be respectful of others' ideas. Most importantly, pay attention to the details, and don't get too comfortable in your routines. Reviewing a process we have completed a hundred times may seem monotonous, but this is usually the window that opens for mistakes to happen because we are too comfortable in the repetition.

The Art of Giving Feedback

The Main Course

Feedback is the core of cultivating a culture of continuous improvement within our teams. Not just a tool to point out mistakes, but a method to support growth in everyone involved.

When delivered correctly, it will positively impact team morale and engagement. When executed incorrectly, it drives down productivity and the motivation to produce results. Getting it right isn't a guessing game that should be done haphazardly. You must be intentional in delivery, timeliness, structure, and outcome at all times.

I have always been a fan of 'Manager Tools'. From a young age, first stepping into management, I found myself researching how I could improve my skills as both a manager and a leader. Not only to better myself but to be better for those around me.

One of the knowledge wells I continually found myself returning to was a podcast called '*Manager Tools*'.

The co-founders of *Manager Tools*, Mark Horstman and Mike Auzenne, are both graduates of the United States Military Academy at West Point. My thought process around feedback culture derive from what I learned at *Manager Tools*. When you make the time, check it out and make the same personal development investment.

We suck at giving feedback.

I'm not talking about the Gordon Ramsey yelling in the ears of new chefs about their terrible sauce until they bleed as feedback. I think we do that just fine.

I'm talking about giving feedback on specific behavior that helps correct future behavior.

Like management, leadership, and coaching styles, there are several types of feedback styles.

1. Informal - a spontaneous comment that occurs at any moment for any reason, whether the receiver is wanting it or not.
2. Formal - feedback that is planned, structured and scheduled in a consistent setting with both parties understanding the goal of meeting.
3. Constructive - feedback that is observation based, with specific and actionable comments.
4. Summative - feedback aimed at helping one understand how they did over a long period of time.
5. Empathetic - an emotional-based feedback used to show caring about one's situation and how it effects their performance.

The list is long as the personality types that are used for each feedback style. But let us not lean on a specific style, just the mechanism of performing feedback better.

The way that most feedback is given in our industry is by observing something that is wrong, telling the person why, reminding them what the correct standard is, and what will happen if they keep doing it incorrectly.

Example: *"Billy, you keep burning the garlic before you add in the onions. You should only brown the garlic, then add in the onion, and finish with white wine. If you keep doing that, the dish will taste burnt and it'll be ruined."*

In your mind, Coach K couldn't have done it any better.

In Billy's mind, you're an a-hole. Only because what you said and what Billy heard were two different things.

Let's take a look at the mechanisms for giving good feedback:

1. Ask to give feedback
2. Describe the situation
3. Describe the behavior
4. Describe the consequences
5. Assess the event subjectively
6. Share future expectations

In looking at this list one may think that the above example with Billy hits 4 of the 6 items and should be good enough. Not so fast my friend. Let's break this replay down in slow motion and check out what the eyes (and ears) didn't catch.

The only thing Billy heard as he was deep in thought was that you think his dishes are burnt and ruined. Part of the art of giving feedback is understanding that people will react more to negative feedback than to positive. Meaning, if a person lost a $20 bill while washing their clothes, the emotion would resonate longer and stronger than if a person finds a random $20 bill in the washing machine.

These emotion and reaction stages are also true in your restaurant. Just like the burnt garlic ruins the sauce for the chicken piccata, harsh words ruin the atmosphere of getting things done the right way for the right reasons.

The first step in feedback is ask. Yes, I literally mean ask them if you can give them some feedback. This does a few things. First, it prepares the one mentally to receive it. As we are all lost in thought throughout the day, there are times when someone says something and because we were not prepared to listen, we hear something totally different. This miscommunicated statement can at times sour the moment, ruining the timing of information about to be delivered. After that the feedback, no matter how positively worded, is rendered ineffective in its delivery no matter how you repeat it. The only thing they remember is what they *thought* you said. Second, it also gives them the chance to say 'no', which in a professional setting is very rare. If they do say no, there is more going on than just burnt garlic that needs to be addressed.

Next, describe the situation without describing the person. This a tough one, but you want to take the me-vs-you or the blame game out of the conversation from the beginning. In the example above, Billy's context was used 5 times. 'Billy' was used once and 'you' was said four times. That's the equivalent of taking your finger and jabbing Billy in the chest five times during your interaction.

A better intro to the feedback, after asking to give it, could be, "Billy, I noticed that some of the best sauce has the garlic browned, then right before it gets too dark, the onion is added then finished with white wine. Matter of fact, I've tasted yours when you've done it that way. It's always been perfect."

Not only have you described the situation, but you've also described the behavior of what success looks like, and the fact that you've seen Billy be successful before in building the sauce.

To round out the conversation, the next part of the exchange would finish with the consequences and future expectations. Let's take a look at the improved interaction in full.

Example 2: "Billy, can I give you some feedback? I noticed that some of the best sauce has the garlic browned, then right before it gets too dark, the onion is added then finished with white wine. Matter of fact, I've tasted yours when you've done it that way. It's always been perfect. Next time, reduce the flame a little, be patient, and look for the browning queues while having the onion ready to add. If you need help, let me know and I'll walk you through how to stage it. Show me your next one and we'll make sure you have it right. Thanks."

The second, although wordier, corrects the future behavior. We can assume at this moment Billy isn't cursing you under his breath. And, Coach K could not have done it any better.

In live replay we don't get the time to always formulate our thoughts and words perfectly, but practice in being cognizant of how we say things and what we want the outcome to be makes the conversation more natural.

Mastering the delivery of group feedback should be handled with a different approach. Although rare, group feedback has underlying parameters to help it be effective. First, group feedback should be given when the feedback involves more than two individuals on a team that relies on each other for performance output. For example, if Steve, Ray, and Chris are unable to meet deadlines on tasks because Michael is producing results, all four individuals should be included in the feedback moment.

You as a leader would only be able to speak in detail about what Steve, Ray, and Chris are going through to Michael if the three are there to give specifics on behavior and situations firsthand. At the same time, Michael should be able to answer questions about his performance directly to his team.

The group feedback however should only be in the presence of those directly involved and should not include others outside of that circle in order to not become a spectacle. Lastly, all parties should know in advance of the feedback session in the same way you would ask an individual.

Another type of feedback style is called the AIR feedback model. The acronym AIR stands for Action, Impact, Request. It's a simple framework that focuses on making a SMART (Specific, Measurable, Achievable, Relevant, Time-Bound) request towards an individual. By naming the action observed, the impact on the person or thing from that action, and requesting, 'Would you be willing to_____?', in a SMART format, you are more so able to change the future behavior of the individual.

Using this style, you still have to be conscious of:

1. Describing the behavior, not the personality of the

person
2. Not labeling the person
3. Make sure it is performance focused
4. Be clear and to the point
5. Ask to give feedback
6. Make the feedback timely

The last type of feedback most commonly used is the 360-feedback model. This style is typically reserved for feedback on managers and leaders in many industries. It is also a great tool for your assistant managers, shift leaders, and trainers under you. Less an in-the-moment feedback tool, it's more so a technique of gathering feedback from multiple sources to get a better picture of one's performance with different perspectives to build a better overview of a particular area.

No matter the feedback style, the goal is still the same. To instill a culture of continuous learning in your four walls through the encouragement of feedback and changed behaviors. That is the positive change that everyone can look forward to.

The Takeaway

Mastering the art of giving feedback in our industry strengthens our competencies in empathy, clarity, and committing to continuous improvement. Recognize feedback as an opportunity for growth rather than criticism. This can foster an environment where team members feel motivated to enhance their skills versus being afraid to show them. By instilling this mindset, managers can create a positive feedback system that contributes to the team's overall success.

Effective feedback hinges on timeliness and specificity. Deliver feedback promptly, allowing employees to connect their actions with specific outcomes in the moment. Be specific about the observed actions and areas needing improvement, then provide clear guidance. This technique ensures that team members understand expectations and can make targeted adjustments to their performance.

Leaning equally on both positive reinforcement and constructive criticism is crucial. As a manager and leader, you should acknowledge strengths and achievements before addressing areas for improvement. This balanced approach creates an atmosphere where team members feel valued and supported, fostering a more receptive environment for constructive feedback.

Choosing the right setting for feedback sessions is also vital. Provide a private and distraction-free space where open communication can thrive. Start with positive feedback, provide constructive criticism, and end with positive reinforcement, creating a more empathetic and collaborative interaction.

Handling negative feedback requires a focus on behavior rather than personality. When addressing performance issues, concentrate on specific actions that need improvement. Additionally, managers should not just point out problems but offer constructive solutions. By working together to create action plans for improvement, managers empower employees and reinforce a commitment to ongoing support and development.

The Angle

Always be positive. People that love what they do generally are meaning to do the right thing. If there's an issue it most often was a mistake. Mistakes happen and being positive during the conversation, I believe, leads to positive change of behavior. With the right team everyone should be aligned in a common goal, so feedback (positive or negative) should be received well.

-Sean Keyes – VP Design & Construction, Focus Brands, Lancaster PA

I am very open, honest and forthcoming. If someone is struggling with another colleague or subordinate, I bring everyone together and get it all out on the table as difficult as it may be for everyone. Most people struggle with speaking openly and honestly in front of each other but it's the only method that truly works. If they won't speak up

I'll say "Michael you're struggling with the way Ken is speaking down to you and I've heard him speak condescending to you, isn't that true? How does that make you feel"? That will start the conversation rolling and then you just play mediator.

   -Mike Moore – Hospitality Executive, NY NY

When I provide feedback, I focus on how this information is going to help the receiver. Asking questions is a great way to lead someone to a conclusion they may not have come to without guidance and support.

   -Julie Thompson – Senior Instructional Design, Zaxby's Grill, Atlanta GA

Always begin with given them a "Charitable assumption" as we don't know what they may be going thru at that time and to listen with the intent to understand.

   -Gerald Pulsinelli – CEO, Viva Chicken, Charlotte NC

The reciprocation of feedback varies from person to person, this is why I try to always provide a bit of positive with the not so positive and bring solutions for improvement along with how the feedback is linked to our company mission and employee development. I've found sharing feedback in a timely manner is most effective along with tailoring the message with strategic facts rather than personal opinions. Finally, I make feedback conversational where both parties come up with solutions. This helps create ownership, investment and accountability.

   -Ranita Bullock – Corporate Catering Manager, Brock & Company, Inc.

A technique I learned earlier in my career was referred to as SBI . . . Situation, Behavior and Impact. What is going on and what point do you need to get across (situation)? What behavior is needed (or needs changed) (Behavior)? What impact is desired or expected (Impact)? It's pretty simple, but as I prepare to communicate or coach a team member, I try and ensure my point of view and message is clear in those three areas.

-Coley O'Brien – *Chief People Officer, The Wendy's Company, Dublin OH*

Feedback is the breakfast of champions.

-Ken Blanchard – *Author, Business Consultant, Motivational Speaker*

What is the shortest word in the English language that contains the letters: abcdef? Answer: feedback. Don't forget that feedback is one of the essential elements of good communication.

–Anonymous

Always LEAD WITH POSITIVE. Point out the Positive. Catch them doing something RIGHT! There are two ways to potty train a puppy. Do you follow the puppy around the house with a rolled-up newspaper and wait for him/her to use the bathroom on the carpet and then "pop" them on the bum with the rolled-up newspaper and say "no" or "bad dog"? This is a terrible experience for the puppy, and they learn to fear you quickly. In fact, maybe they don't want to be around you at all. Or is it better to proactively take the puppy outside every two hours and wait for them to use the bathroom and then CELEBRATE SUCCESS with the puppy? Great job! Way to go potty outside! Then give them a treat every time they use the bathroom outside. The puppy will catch on quickly. This is kind of a silly example, I know, but the puppy will respond way better to the positive reinforcement. The puppy wants to please people around him/her. When you walk into a store, or you kick off your meetings, always spend the first 15 minutes CELEBRATING SUCCESS. Maybe someone received a high score on a Food Safety Audit that week? Maybe someone received 3 five star reviews that week. Get in the practice of recording and logging great achievements within your group every day or week, and then CELEBRATE SUCCESS by reciting these achievements in front of their peers or their team. Leading with positivity and celebrating success will soon trickle down through your organization. You will soon find your GMs celebrating success with their subordinates, thus leading to a positive work culture.

   -Steve Taylor *– Managing Member, CapQueen3 LLC, Charlotte NC*

Closing The Gap

The Main Course

In this chapter we're going to talk through the frustrations that can happen between customer and operator, what causes the gap in those frustrations, and how to close that gap. Although both customer and operator are in the same four walls, they can have very different views on what a good or even great experience is. By the end of this short chapter, I hope you have one to two ways to permanently close the gap in your business and know how to view it from many eyes instead of just one set.

You live the two-wheel life. Do you know what that means? That means that although your car has four wheels, you are pulling into the parking lot at work so fast that you're literally on two wheels. Driver door open, left foot out, big toe dragging as you're pulling into the parking space.

And do you know why? Because your phone has blown up from the 12th text message with the sixth picture about last nights close. And, your truck company called. Since they are short on drivers, they had to change your route again, so your truck order is now due 30 minutes ago. Lastly, payroll emailed. Someone forgot to clock out last weekend and they can't process payroll until you log into the portal (we love the portal) and correct their hours.

Hence, your two-wheel life. And, you can't even remember the details of the last half mile before you pulled in. Scary. Come to think about it, even if it wasn't one of those Wednesdays, you normally don't remember the last half mile of your trip in to work. Crazy how that is, but we'll touch on that later. Let's get back to your big toe…

…big toe dragging as you're pulling into the parking space. *Screech*! You get out, car door barely closes, and you're speed walking 90 mph into the doors. As you head inside, you see some guests in line, so you assist with the front counter for a few moments. Then you head back through the kitchen to reduce their clog, place the truck order off memory, knock out payroll, then '*Phew*', you can now do your job.

But, it's too late. Your heart is pumping a 90 mph and you are officially on fire. You are in your groove. Making laps like NASCAR, giving feedback, pointing things out to clean, touching tables, completing checklists. Girl, you are on FIRE!

Finally, after working your triple-double for the day, you get home, give yourself two high fives, and somehow fall asleep. The next morning you wake up to that lovely email tone.

Ding.

It's a guest survey. You got a 2 out of 5 on 'Clean' from their visit yesterday.

You just about flip the nightstand.

"They lyin'!".

Your cat runs frantically out of the bedroom.

"I was there all day!", you say to yourself frantically. "I pulled a triple-double! I was lapping like NASCAR. Giving my feedback.

Pointing my fingers. Feeling up tables. I was on fire. There's no way my restaurant wasn't clean… Must by Jaime that I fired last week. He's trying to set me up with fake surveys!"

But the fact is, there's a gap between what an operator sees and what a customer sees, and it is more prevalent than we realize. The operator has, what I call, 20/20 vision. No, not that good vision. Over half of us wear glasses just to spot a cruise ship.

Twenty-twenty vision is that we're always looking 20 feet out and 20 feet wide. We're looking for the next fire. The next thing to go wrong, maybe even someone doing something right. Our head is on a constant swivel scanning the room like the terminator. At an average 5-foot-6 inch height, your view of things is seen walking at a fast pace from 5 feet above for only a few moments as we move to look at the next shiny object.

The 20/20 vision practice is practical and helpful when it comes to the many moving parts of our business. When done right, it helps us to view equipment that may be out of place, inactive timers for product or processes, cold or hot holding product sitting on counters, low stock products, unfilled orders, or even out of place team members.

Because of the high wattage lights generally used in kitchen areas, we can also get a view of items that need to be cleaned and/or repaired. In a fast paced, constantly moving environment, the 20/20 vision approach can be helpful.

However, your customer's view is much different.

In the customer's perspective, they've been on the go all day, with personal chores or at work. They get to our restaurant and finally have a few moments to pause and relax. They pull in to the parking lot nice and slow. Obviously checking to see if someone lives here, or if the overgrown shrubs and trash means it may not be open. As they're walking up to the door, they're checking the slit by the door handle to see if the door's locked so they don't dislocate their shoulder by pulling on a locked door. A trick customers learned at the peak of COVID.

When they see that it's unlocked, they feel like they struck gold because they're tired of eating in their cars out of paper bags from their dashboard. As they walk in, it's like seeing something or someplace new for the first time all over again.

By design, most dining rooms are slightly dimmer than the outside or the kitchen area, for ambiance. The customers iris will naturally increase in size due to lower light, taking in more detail as they scan the area. They see more!

Most customers have what I like to call 18/3 vision versus the operators 20/20 vision. The customer is intently focused on items that are 18 inches from their nose, and take notice of most things that are 3-feet high and lower, especially when sitting in a chair. The most comfortable level when sitting is with a relaxed neck and leveled chin, eyes comfortably looking forward or slightly down. At these angles your customer has a much different view of the operator's world in the same four walls. This is where 'The Gap' is at its widest.

Even from the outside, it's hard for you to remember the last 1/2 mile before arriving to your job. As an operator when you're pulling up, there's a subconscious mental exercise your mind completes right before heading into battle. It drowns out the visual items it sees everyday and focuses on the unknown stresses that may lay ahead inside the building. That's because you are thinking through what you have to get done for the day, who is going to call out, what didn't get done from the prior night, and a million other things.

The closer you get to work, the less you see on the ride in, and the more your mind is on autopilot bringing you in to the last few feet. The front and side curbs from the roadway are almost non-existent in your mind.

When you picture work, you may envision the sidewalk next to the exterior walls, a few bushes, then your mind go straight to the people, process, and equipment. This is where the gap continues.

When the customer pulls up, it's a mental exercise of 'is this place open?'. Does it look like they're open for business? Did the parking lot get cleaned showing they are expecting customers? Are the lights on showing they are open? A million and one things go through the customers mind as well, but most of it pertains to cues on the outside.

As the guest walks in, it's a sigh of relief that they will get served.

As you walk in, it's a focus on people, product, and processes, or the first administrative items that needs to get completed. All of this is the dueling lateral world of the gap.

Let's do an exercise. I want you to choose the three most popular tables in your dining room or lobby. The one's that get sat the most by your customers (and probably by your employees). Have a seat at one and get relaxed. Now imagine that your food you ordered is on the table. Stare at a spot 18 inches from your nose on the table where your food would normally be.

As you're staring, count to 10 slowly. You will notice your eyes begin to pick up detail on the tabletop, as if you were picking up detail on your steak or salad. Now, after a few moments, as if your stomach is getting full, begin to lean back in your chair and let your eyes slowly draw from the spot on the table, over the edge of the table across from you, and across the room. Don't let your eyes go any higher than 3-feet, then bring them back down to the floor directly in front of you.

As your eye adjusts, and after 2–3 seconds, let your chin draw your head slowly left to right as your eyes bounce from ground level to no higher that 3-feet as you span back and forth across the room slowly. Since you're at a reduced speed of life, versus 90 mph, you will begin to pick up more detail on things both near and far. From the 18-inch adjustment dust particles seem as large as boulders from this view.

Now, change seats at the very same table, face the opposite direction and complete the same exercise. No cheating! Don't sit down and start staring across the room. Have a seat, stare at the table for 10 seconds, then act as if your stomach is getting full and let your eyes float up to no more than 3 feet high and slowly pan from left to right, getting a little wider with each pass. You will notice that the exact same table provides a very different view on all things whether furniture, ledges, chair backs and legs, to windows and more.

Now change tables to the second most sat, and the third most sat. Sitting in different seats and repeating the exercise from the beginning for each one. You will see the gap in the customer view and operator view, and begin to understand why your experience at times differs from your guest. That gap comes from the lower height and longer looks of items at very short distances with a heart rate that is substantially slowed. This shows the clean, organized, dirty, and disheveled nature of things that we tend to overlook.

To expand this exercise, listen intently to the background, employee, or kitchen noise at each table. Feel for the air conditioning vents when they come on. Listen to volume of the music or employees, and the ease or difficulty of holding a conversation. These are all things that may not be considered as clean or not clean, but can add or take away from the experience your team has worked hard in creating.

Now that we see the gap, the question is how do we begin to close it?

These days, with ongoing staffing and training challenges, most managers find themselves locked into a functional position during peak periods. This ensures throughput is at its maximum for your business. But this is still the best time of day to get a read on true customer experience in your business. These next steps should be completed during peak periods in traffic and sales.

The first step in closing the gap is scheduling yourself to do a walk of the entire lot of your business once a week. Start at the very front right side of your building next to the road or highway. Remember, this is how your customer views your business even if they are not choosing to stop that day. Take the walk along the right-side edge of your lot and complete the walk to the back left, then along the left side back to the front, taking notes of what takes away of adds to the entire experience. This should be completed at least once a week, if not daily.

Completing this outdoor walk is not effective prior to opening or during slow periods. You want to see what the customer sees when it is the highest peak of business hours. This is when the most advertising of who you are or aren't is being done. Think about TV ads. Do they charge more or less when more people are watching? That is because the highest ROI is with more viewers during the peak periods, not before the show even starts.

A few keys to getting this completed is to first schedule yourself to do this. Don't let anything else derail the walk. If needed, bring an employee or assistant with you and use it for development time. Second, slow down. This is not a fast task designed to be checked off as completing. It's also not a speed walk around the edge of your lot. It is something to be in tune with the landscaping, grease spots, micro trash, and more as you face your building from all angles.

Take into account all things outdoors in this process. Leaking down spots from the roof. Dumpster pad areas. Even back dock and sidewalk staining from employee shoes. Lastly, take notes and/or pictures. I would love to say that we all have steel traps resting on our shoulders, but we know we do not. This gives you a point of reference as other items may come up on the walk you were not expecting.

The next step in continuing to close the gap is scheduling yourself once or twice a month, or even week, to make observations from your dining room or lobby. The most difficult thing about doing this correctly is the fact that we are programmed to jump in when something is not going right. Trust me, you will see plenty of things not going right during these observations, but you have to resist the urge to jump in and save the team. If you're that concerned about not being in a position for 20-30 minutes, what is happening on your day off when you're not in the building at all?

Let the process of ownership from your team and observations from the customers view take its course. Take notes, teach it to your team, and close the gap in your business. Always remember, the destination of a great running restaurant is only a few steps outside of your normal work path. And, slowing down will actually get you there faster.

The Takeaway

Our routines put us at a disadvantage to be locked into viewing the same things consistently. Even though it feels like every day brings us a new unexpected challenge, this can adversely force us to view only a few common things consistently at a deep level. This is good, but not great. Break out of that mold.

View your business from the angle of your customer, figuratively and literally. Start with the trip in and view it from the curb lines. Make sure the exterior looks like someone does live (work) there. Make note of what takes away or adds to that view. Then execute, not just make a plan for it. This should be done weekly if not daily.

Pay attention more closely to the last half mile driving up to your business and compare your building to everyone around you, not just other restaurants. How do their lots compare to yours. Now find ways to stand out above theirs.

When entering into the building pay attention to the customer sight lines. What is it that they see, hear and feel? Make adjustments to this.

Slow down during this process and let the low-level lighting adjust your eyes. 20-feet wide and 20-feet away doesn't work well in the customer viewing areas. Pay more attention to things that are 18 inches away and three feet down and lower. This is the natural angle of a sitting customer.

Loop your team into this especially on the outdoor walk and at the most popular tables. This will help close the gap in the customer expectations and operator execution. This exercise and approach should not be overlooked or skipped over ever. Some tactics in other chapters are 'good to do's'. Skipping this one will cause frustration with your customers, your team, and yourself.

The Angle

Closing the gap between guest expectations and operator execution takes intentional training, planning, and empathy. You must not only put yourself in the position of the guest, but also be able to train and coach your team to do the same. It requires continual focus on your people so they stay motivated to focus on your guests.

-Julie Thompson – Senior Instructional Design, Zaxby's Grill, Atlanta GA

Always put ourselves in the seat of the guest, see through their eyes and ask ourselves what would I would expect from our dining experience.

-Gerald Pulsinelli – CEO, Viva Chicken, Charlotte NC

Get closer than ever to your customers. So close that you tell them what they need well before they realize it themselves.

-Steve Jobs – Founder, Apple Inc., Palo Alto CA

If you're competitor-focused, you have to wait until there is a competitor doing something. Being customer-focused allows you to be more pioneering.

-Jeff Bezos – Founder, Amazon, Seattle WA

What gets measured gets managed! Customer Experience quantified is 90% or greater all the time. So, we generally would close the gap between customer perception vs. reality by tracking the internal metrics of each restaurant. What was the score of the last 3rd-party Food Safety Audit? What was the score of the last county food safety inspection?

1. *What was the score of the last unannounced Franchisor inspections?*
2. *What is the average of the customer satisfaction scores over the last 3 months? (Nineties are NICE, eighties are unacceptable!)*

3. *How many 5 star google reviews have you had in the last 3 months?*
4. *Once we aggregate all of these scores, how does your stack rank compare against the rank of your peers in our system?*

How does the stack rank of our system compare to that of the entire franchise?

We can close the gap by improving all of these scores individually first. You really start to get a good picture of how your operations are going by aggregating all of the metrics.

-Steve Taylor – Managing Member, CapQueen3 LLC, Charlotte NC

Using The Power of Influence

The Main Course

You hear these 4 words all too often in our industry:

'The Power of Influence'.

These 4 words are used too loosely and, this 'power' and tactic, should be used only at the right times. The caution around influence is that you truly have no power or control over it despite the famous slogan. It comes and goes like the wind, enabling itself to whoever it chooses, and it does not care about highlighting the best of one's abilities. Influence moves people to model another person in many traits, not just the positive ones.

Influence is also addictive to the one who tries to yield it, even those with the best intentions. Those wielding influence to make positive change gets a surprise boost of unforeseen adrenaline when they find out the task they set was successful. What makes this dangerous is when others see you successful in influence and bring other items or decisions for you to sway with benefits that may be shrouded with bad intent.

Our hospitality industry is one that is weighted heavily by people performing duties to the right standard in situations where supervision is at a distance. Hence, the use of the term, The Power of Influence.

With all that said, that's why one of the keys in this book is dedicated to understanding the true understanding and power of influence. Not just the influence you think you left behind for others to mimic and act on. But also, the unintended influence that you and others may not realize lingers for far longer than we hope. In this key you will hear me use the term persuasion and influence interchangeably as both are very similar.

So, let's front load the solution to save you some time, since this is how this book is formatted. In order to use 'The Power of Influence' correctly you must actively engage in being conscious to how you treat each and every person in your workplace, whether they work directly for you or not.

Contrary to popular belief, it is not telling someone how you want them to act or behave. It isn't showing them when you think they are looking, or listening, how you want them to copy your style, or follow your lead. It's the consistent practice of knowing how you're impressing on them, especially when they are not looking. Because usually, that's when they are paying the most attention.

In 1959, social psychologists John French and Bertram Raven conducted a study on power, how some leaders use or wield power, and why for some it resonates many years after working for or with certain leaders. During this study, French and Raven categorized Power to 5 different sections:

1. Legitimate Power – the belief that a person has the formal right to make demands, and to expect others to be compliant and obedient. Example: King, Queen, high level executive.
2. Reward Power – the practice of one person's ability to compensate another for compliance. Example: Giving or taking away of finances for tasks completed.
3. Expert Power – the result of a person's high level of skill and knowledge. Example: Professor, Doctor, Lawyer, Consultant.
4. Referent Power – the result of a person's perceived attractiveness, worthiness and right to others' respect. Example: Being friends with a hero or well-liked associate, to which you also receive favoritism.
5. Coercive Power – the belief that a person can punish others for noncompliance. Example: Threats of force to gain compliance. Authorities.

After this study was completed, six years later, a sixth and separate category was added called 'informational power' which is directly linked to social communication and the power of social influence. This helped to define the term social influence as - *'a change in the belief or attitude of a person resulting from the action of another person'*.

From this spurned many tactics, practices and techniques on how to hone one's skill in organizational communications to others. You can thank the late addition of this sixth category to billions of books purchased, videos viewed, and courses attended by millions of professionals over the last 6-7 decades.

I already know the question you're asking yourself. 'How's

this going to make my dishwasher wash dishes faster during my closing hours?'

It won't.

This key is focused more so on your team making the right choices when you are or aren't in the building, not on increased throughput.

The way to get the highest return on investment in the power of influence is to use it for good. It's a shame that one must state that, but that is the best foundational approach of this tactic. The repercussions in using it with bad intent can be extremely damaging shown in many case studies.

Let's view influence as 6 tactical principles to be used sparingly. World renowned psychologist Dr. Robert Cialdini has defined 6 universal truths or principles around influence or persuasion. By using the 6 principles of persuasion set by Dr. Cialdini, leaders such as yourself will begin to elevate their influence levels to unimaginable heights. Let's take a look at the 6 principles and how you can apply them to your professional environment.

Principle of Reciprocity - the principle of reciprocity is pretty simple: what you put out will come back around to reward you later. Where some get frustrated is the want of 'immediate and even' reciprocity rewards, and they want it to be announced and flaunted for all to see. This is definitely the wrong approach. A mindset to be in when using reciprocity is that what you give or do for one individual may come back in favor from another that may have heard or seen your good gesture. The timing of this can be of an infinite span as well. Next month, next quarter, next fiscal year. The laws of power have no boundaries. They will give and receive at their own pace.

Some ideas in reciprocity are awarding someone for doing good, even if there isn't a contest. Tidying up the office at every close, no matter who opens the next morning. Writing 'Thank You' on any payroll envelope for those that don't get a direct deposit. Even making eye contact when thanking someone after their shift is over, even if they didn't stay longer than needed. Lastly, getting reports in a day earlier than asked so that the one that has to review or approve them has extra time to do so.

Principle of Scarcity - people want more of anything when they can only have less of it due to demand. Now this principle teeters on the edge of 'Good' and 'Gray'. It's hard to not see this as a dangling carrot technique, but when used in the proper context, it can fuel motivation to get positive things completed. By holding dear to things that are in high demand, the opportunity to motivate others to react can produce great results. For example, creating marketing of having only a few more items to be sold of something that cannot be found by competitors. Featuring a hotel room that will give a premium view of an event that only happens annually. Another example is advertising to your crew a number of limited leadership roles in your business. These roles may come with additional benefits, PTO, preferred schedules and more. There may be a certain window that you accept internal applicants that meet a certain criterion based on performance. Getting creative with the scarcity principle can get out of hand quickly, so you must be sure to use it correctly and sparingly.

Principle of Authority - hearing about a random fact from someone standing next to you in a kitchen holds little water. Especially if it's your first day and you've never met this person before. But if they were introduced to you as Sarah – with 15 years of culinary experience, that graduated from the CIA and recently did an apprenticeship under Bobby Flay for 3 years, you may hang on every word she says. In the terms of you using Authority from your own point of view, it would sound narcissistic to introduce yourself to everyone with your long list of accolades. (Please don't do that.)

One way is to always have someone else introduce you with a brief accolade. This still may border conceit but in the right fashion can yield the same result. Another way is when introducing your team to always note a recognition showing the depth of every around you. This gives an underlying tone of your own accomplishments because of the depth that is around you. Overly doing the authority principle can yield to an environment of entitlement. This approach must be used lightly.

Principle of Consistency - this principle is the easiest to state, but hardest to do for some leaders. If you say you are going to do something, do it. Once upon a time in a brand I worked with many years ago in the Carolina's there was a manager having trouble with getting their team to complete tasks and items that she asked them to do.

Manager - "Jason, it seems like no one does what I assign them, even when I threaten discipline. It's like pulling teeth but they just don't care."

Me - "I have a question. Do you do what you say you're

going to do?"

Manager - "What?"

Me - "When you tell a team member or manager to make sure they do 'X', or 'Y' would be the repercussions. Do you do 'Y' if 'X' doesn't happen?"

Manager - *Long Pause…* "No"

Me - "Well, if you don't do what you say you're going to do, why should they do what you tell them when you don't keep your word?"

The point isn't that making threats should be your go to. It is whatever we say we are going to do, we need to be consistent and do it. Not just with ultimatums for failed tasks, but with holding standards, fulfilling promises, even getting things complete when something comes up, we believe is out of our control. Lastly, we need to stay consistent with the environment we create for our teams, customers and brand. The more consistency we create for others around us and they know what to expect daily, the more we can get others to commit to holding the same standards, fulfilling the same promises, completing the same items, and creating the same consistency for others around them too.

The final piece that puts icing on the principle cake is making the above commitment in a public setting when appropriate. By doing so, it brings on the same feeling of a Double Dog Dare. Because when it's public, it's written in stone. Which makes one ensure the commitment is upheld. And when completed, the layer of influence or persuasion is that much stronger and ready to be used for the right purposes.

Principle of Social Proof - social proof is informing someone that people similar to them, in their exact situation, when given a choice, has chosen a specific option a certain percentage of the time.

Hotels use this with reusing towels when staying in a hotel room for more than one night. This helps reduce water usage and labor by washing all towels in the hotel after being used once. The card says something along the lines of, 'By reusing your towels you help to conserve water for the environment'.

When guests read the card, studies found that a certain percentage of people will reuse their towels more times than when the card is not in the bathroom. When they changed the wording to say '75% of our guests reuse their towels in order to conserve water for the environment', a higher number of guests reuse their towels in response. When the wording is then changed to say '75% of guests that use this room reuse their towels in order to conserve water for the environment', an even higher number of guests reuse their towel due to the social queue of 'I should be doing of what everyone else is doing'.

Let's use this principle for computer-based training in your restaurant. By telling a new hire they need to complete the 4 Core Training Assessments for their position, you may get a 50% completion rate if it is self-paced. If you have a sign next to the schedule and the training laptop that read, '75% of our employees completed their 4 Core Training Assessments the first 2 weeks they were hired', what do you think the completion rate would be? What if you changed the wording to '75% of our employees that were promoted in the first 9 months completed all Core Training Assessments for every position the first 3 months of being hired', what do you think the completion rate of the first 4 and more assessments would be then?

You could use the same principle for pre-bussing tables to increase tips, reduced recooks to decrease food cost, and much more.

Principle of Liking - I will preface this principle before getting into the definition and examples with, you don't need to be liked to be the boss. But it helps.

Please don't confuse this as a tactic that involves you putting a like-o-meter on a spreadsheet and figuring out ways to get your average up across your entire team.

The true crux of this principle is, when a person is relatable with someone else, they tend to cooperate more towards a common goal. This goes back to engaging with your team through one-on-ones to build a long-lasting relationship. Although your end goal isn't to be liked, you do end up becoming a leader that shares common hobbies or interests giving common ground to build on. Another way to solidify relationship building is by giving genuine compliments at appropriate times. This is very effective before entering into any form of negotiations or challenging times.

Be sure to find ways to connect with your team even if you

find yourself more transactional in nature. To get some of the best transactions completed there needs to be foundation of common ground.

Be careful not to have too much focus on this principle too much throughout your day or year. Use liking as a foundational approach to help build your relationships especially during the beginning of one's tenure. Then lean into being courteous and having common ground while remaining professional in your role to receive the best results.

The Takeaway

Influence is not a straightforward tactic. There are many uncontrollable aspects to its power that will enable itself when it so chooses. That's not to say it isn't an important method to study and enable when possible. We just need to understand that it's not as simple as we think.

The studies around influence 60-70 years ago show us that persuasion at work can still be effective today. To do so effectively we should be conscious of a few principles. These principles will help us understand how our persuasion can sway the choice of others.

Although not your everyday focus, Reciprocity, Authority, Scarcity, Consistency, Social Proof, and Liking are all factors that help affect decision making in ourself and those around us. By understanding this you can use them to your advantage in sales building, people development and much more. The laws and rules of management, leadership, and coaching still apply to your everyday world. These principles just help to underline the effort and success rate in reaching our goals.

All 6 principles boil down to one word, communication. Both verbally and non-verbally. It's not always what we say and show that others will mimic. It's also the times we think no one is listening or watching that those around us are watching the most, even our customers.

It is impossible not to influence others even if we consciously choose not to. Your power on influence is constant and ever changing. By creating a consistent environment, you will more likely create the influence you seek with good intent. The caution around influence is it also powers itself when you choose to ignore it's foundation. We all ride a thin edge of not letting its focus consume our mission, nor ignoring its underlying current in those around us.

The Angle

Influence is the greatest untapped power within any organization. It is an internally developed trait within an individual, but it's derived from a simple premise- respect. The influencers in your organization regardless of title or position command the respect of people at multiple levels; so much so that people actually seek their counsel.

*-**Pat Peterson** - Senior VP of Restaurants, Wagamama USA, NY NY*

Influence all comes down to relationships, no matter what level of the organization you may be. Influence is like tokens at an arcade, you collect them by strengthening your relationships with people over time and then when you need to redeem them for a prize or to play a game, you can easily.

*-**Alan Magee** – VP Marketing & Communications, Empire Portfolio Group, NY NY*

The best lesson in influence is to put a person in a position of indirect vs. direct power. This can be achieved by creating work stream teams with a "lead" or can be created by dotted line relationships. Any opportunity to flex a consensual/influential style vs. command and control is great for the development of leaders in today's business.

*-**Kimberly Grant** – Fortune 100 Director, Performance Food Group, Washington DC*

I would ask them to reflect on a time that someone made them feel special. Once they had that in mind, I would ask them if they would perform at a higher level for that person. Then, I would ask them to think about the techniques that person used to make them feel special and to put together an action plan to put those things into practice.

*-**Paul Macaluso** – President & CEO, Another Broken Egg, Orlando FL*

People I've viewed as being skilled at the art of influencing demonstrated very similar attributes . . . they knew what they were talking about (knowledgeable); they knew how to communicate appropriately their audience (relatable); and people believed what they were saying (trustworthy). I'm not saying those are the only requirements to being good at influencing, but I'm certain you can't be successful at influencing without demonstrating those three attributes.

*-**Coley O'Brien** – Chief People Officer, The Wendy's Company, Dublin OH*

The Wrap Up

This is a book I wish I had at the start of my career. It is not a, 'Do everything I say and it will come out perfectly' novel, but a quick-read guide that can be referenced on specific things I found challenging throughout my week. As I said at the beginning of this book, there's no need to read it from front to back, but if you did, I hope you found the content and layout helpful in its entirety.

The goal is to give managers ideas on how to incorporate delegation and whole team ownership into the everyday fabric of the hospitality industry. By doing this, you are creating a foundation to never lead alone again. To be honest, that's not easy. Although we have many brands that enjoy low turnover and long-term employee stability, the fact is not true for the rest of the industry as a whole. Internal support constantly shifting makes building a core team to support you difficult. But that only underlines the fact that we need enhanced efforts in creating leaders to grow our brands, not just managers.

Leading alone is not easy. It's damn near impossible.

Even after building your core team, you still have to trust to let things go. The best fix for this is learning how to delegate the right items, at the right times, to the right people. But everything cannot be done by anyone. There are specific items that make sense by skill level to train someone to do with ongoing follow-up to ensure correct completion. By using the Delegation Template I provided as a bonus for purchasing this book, you can begin your road to using a systematic approach to delegating the right items on your plate.

Another way to delegate is to separate your restaurant into sections. Create mini businesses within your business. Have catering sales? Make an internal catering head and have them in charge of weekly KPIs to monitor its success. Have digital sales? Create an internal third-party delivery and digital sales lead that monitors system up times, refunds, and driver wait times to help drive revenue increase. Your kitchen operations should always be headed by a BOH leader for costs, organization, and ordering tasks.

All of this starts on day zero with how you bring your teams onboard and orient them with the direction your restaurant is heading in. Try not to solely focus on one position. An introduction to your business should be the same for all levels, from dishwasher to executive chef to bar manager. Link how their role and duties enhance the experience of the customer, both indoors and outdoors. Give them shortcuts to learn the names of their colleagues or verbiage that's used within your business. Make the first 100 days matter with an ongoing celebration of them making the right choice to work for you. Then, reap the return as your team embraces your new hires and helps them grow through group development in their department.

As you're building your teams into mini departments, the data has to flow, be accessible, and be highly visible. Having your team own the data by teaching them where to find it, what is relevant to the team, and most importantly what the goals are. This helps everyone orient in the same direction on a shift-to-shift basis.

The challenge a lot of managers and leaders have is not sharing that data out of fear of the team knowing too much. Or, the manager feels the information would be too distracting or burdensome for hourly employees. We do our team an injustice by not expanding their knowledge in the art of the hospitality business.

If the fear is that the data would be too confusing, break it into bite-sized pieces that's appropriate for their position. Link the data-set with the human element of their position and watch the 'Ah, ha!' moments multiply as real-time learning evolves. Either way, you should expect that the day they leave you, and eventually they all move forward, that they represent working for you at a high level because of the knowledge they have gained on how a business operates.

Then, make time for your team to discuss their internal development. The best environment for people to share their thoughts, ideas, and goals can be different individually. Some may excel in an in-the-moment group setting. Others may need a quiet structured environment to open up. This not only creates time for them to share with you their thoughts and ideas, but for you to give them scheduled updates on how they are growing. End of year or mid-year gotcha moments suck for everyone involved. It causes more confusion than clarity, which is never a good outcome. Commit to engaging with your team individually with a scheduled approach and watch that time invested grow. You'll find that you'll be doing less firefighting, and more 'fire-chiefing'.

As you're structuring your group meetings and one-on-one times, be sure to be organized and steer clear of the data dump. Think about it this way, nothing wastes more time than scheduling of time to be wasted.

Whether scheduling a meeting just to have one, or being ill-prepared, ill-timed, or walking away with no decisions being made, we may as well have had no meeting at all. As a leader in a meeting, you should be talking the least and your team should be presenting the most. You have more than enough time to dump on them throughout the day. Use this time to expand your inner core's ownership of the business of their understanding of how it all connects to the business.

Building onto your team's knowledge and their ownership of

presenting that information expands the mindset of everyone involved. Understanding the three distinct but interchangeable mindsets that create success through Managing, Leading, and Coaching is the vehicle that drives this success. Managing is mastery of keeping systems or projects moving in the right direction, at the right speed speeds, to reach a certain point within a specific budget. Leading is the mastery of a painting a picture of what success or a solution looks like even if there isn't a system or vehicle to get there. Then getting a team to take the next steps before the floor appears because the trust in the vision is beyond measure. And coaching is the mastery of small groups and one-on-ones that helps draw out the inner performance of a team or individual. Applying these mindsets at the appropriate time helps one to be more successful in conversations, organizational challenges, and team development.

At this point, you have introduced your team and yourself to the 5 keys to transforming restaurant managers to hospitality leaders. Mastering your KPIs in order to accurately measure performance. Owner like orientation to bring new hires onboard with a big picture view of the business. Delegation by creating mini-GMs to give yourself time to focus on the B.I.G. rocks. Engaging with your team through one-on-ones to drive higher performance to hit personal and professional goals. And finally choosing how to lead with the right mindset of managing, leading, and coaching. All five of these can be a repeatable systematic focus with your business to help drive ownership, create a never stop training environment, and continually assess the best approach for the next step in everything you do. During one-on-one coaching sessions with leaders, I help walk through the planning and implementation of this model to help drive success in their teams.

Looking at not just the business side but the customer side is also a balancing act covered throughout this book. Closing the gap in customer expectations and operator execution starts outside your four walls, up close and personal, at a much slower rate. This starts at the curb of your building and has you view the entire landscape from all 4 corners routinely. From landscaping, to downspouts, grease stains, and proper use of marketing, completing this walk helps to open the eyes of what operators miss on a daily basis. When walking through guest areas, make note of adds or takes away from the customer experience. Then be in tuned with all items that 3 high and lower as this is the angle most seated guests observe when they are in your building.

As we bring all this to a point, we cannot overlook the power of influence we bring to both our team and customers. Influence is never a straightforward tactic. It attaches itself to whomever it chooses whenever it wants to. It will not only focus on your best qualities, but your worst habits, and project them onto others. By understanding the 6 principles of influence, you can be more conscious of your everyday interactions with not only the ones that work for you, but everyone within your environment. By creating a consistent environment, you will more likely create the influence you seek with good intent. This will help project the positive attributes of influence and yield you the best results.

In the introduction, I talked about how we in the hospitality industry get jealous of our white-collar friends with 9 to 5s and extended college degrees. I think we have to change the way our profession is viewed in the general public's eyes. Too many times our industry is looked at as a side job or a first job for youths before they move on to a 'real' job. In 2022 the restaurant industry alone topped $898 billion in revenue, and the hospitality industry combined with hotels, travel, and airlines hit $4.4 trillion in the same year.

On an income level, by comparison, the average teacher salary[6] in the US in 2022 is the same as the average restaurant manager at $57,000. A principal/professor averages $117k a year, while a restaurant owner/CEO averages anywhere from $300k to $33 million annually. But we still caution kids to not grow up flipping burgers for a living. It looks like the burger flipping business is doing just fine these days.

As you get back to your day, week or shift, just remember this: the toughest voyages in the world need a vessel that's manned by more than one person. The hardest battles in history are fought on many fronts. Even if the battle is lost, someone needs to survive to tell the story. Not everything is won because of

[6] Public School Teacher Salary | Salary.com

mere team mentality, but it gives challenges a higher probability of success when someone is shoulder to shoulder with you. I hope this book helps you to build the strongest boat to resist the toughest war while developing the best team so that you may never lead alone again. Have a successful travel, my friend.

The Angle Anthology

This section is the anthology of all the quotes from each key in order. Every quote you've read will be listed here, as well as some bonus quotes that were not listed in previous chapters. Most quotes are from industry professionals I know and have worked with personally. Other quotes are from famous professionals that have spoken about the keys listed in this book.

I would like to thank all my friends, extended family, and industry professionals that took the time to accept my offer to send most of these quotes in. They took the time to think through each topic and give us all their timeless words for readers to connect with. Your wisdom, experience, and guidance in our industry is beyond measure.

Key #1 – Master Your KPI's

KPI's are gold, you absolutely need them to help align members of an organization towards a goal. Tie those into performance reviews and comp and you send a clear message. Everything can be measured in some way (some clearer than others), but the distraction is the temptation to measure everything; it creates analysis paralysis. Develop measures for anything you want, but keep front line operators focused on the 2-3 metrics that you believe will drive your business results right now. If you try to focus on 10 things, that's actually the antithesis of "focus".

*-**Pat Peterson** - Senior VP of Restaurants, Wagamama USA, NY NY*

One unintended consequence to be aware of; when you focus on a KPI, lower skilled operators become single minded and may do things detrimental to the long-term health of the business to "get the number". You yourself need to know the "cheats" and create guardrails.

*-**Pat Peterson** - Senior VP of Restaurants, Wagamama USA, NY NY*

Most people focus on the top 10% and praise them, then the bottom 10% and shame them. But the results really come from pushing the 80% in between. Think about it, If you had 100 Managers in the system and 10 were nailing it, 10 were failing it; you've got essentially a wash. But if 80 were pushed into doing just a little better than average, their momentum carries huge successes.

*-**Pat Peterson** - Senior VP of Restaurants, Wagamama USA, NY NY*

KPIs help align your team around what matters most and the measures that can quantify progress (or lack thereof) and provide a record of milestone goals and achievements. KPIs should be measured on an absolute basis and trends to see long term results.

Key performance indicators are essential to paving a pathway to desired results especially in an industry that requires constant multi-tasking and is often attempting to reach goals that can conflict with one another. Defining KPIs and clearly communicating a reasonable and attainable goal for each one not only keeps the organization focused on what matters most but helps balance opposing goals. For example, creating a KPI for labor/efficiency and a KPI for sales growth could be counterintuitive if both KPIs have an overly aggressive goal. However, if both are set with reasonable and balanced goals it will keep the organization from pushing too hard in one direction and ultimately damaging overall results.

KPIs with objectives properly selected, communicated clearly, and progress systematically shared, keep an organization focused through the multitude of distractions. In addition, clearly defined KPIs allow identification of progress and celebration of wins on the path to success which is critical to keeping the team engaged.

*-**Paul Baldasaro** – COO, Taco Mac, Atlanta GA*

Key #2 - Owner Like Orientation

Empathy is the most important tool in my toolbox. Looking at a situation from someone else's perspective completely changes how I respond to them. During onboarding and orientation, my focus is on understanding the employee's current situation. This enables me to put them at ease, ask questions, and make them comfortable through the process.

*-**Julie Thompson** – Senior Instructional Design, Zaxby's Grill, Atlanta GA*

Each member of the management team is responsible for weekly check ins with the new team member. The GM maybe responsible for the first 30 days, the KM may have as their Area of Responsibility the next 30 days and so on so the new team member is set for succeed along the way.

> -*Gerald Pulsinelli* – *CEO, Viva Chicken, Charlotte NC*

I truly believe that onboarding is an art. Each new employee brings with them a potential to achieve and succeed. To lose the energy of a new hire through poor onboarding is an opportunity lost.

> -*Sarah Wetzel* – *Director of Human Resources, engage:BDR*

The importance of onboarding is significantly increased these days since the average turnover at work is less than four years and lifetime employment strategies are out of date.

> -*Reid Hoffman,* *Ben Casnocha and Chris Yeh* – *Authors of "The Alliance"*

We want to focus on creating a memorable experience for the new hire in the first year rather than processing them in the first few weeks.

> -*Cheryl Hughey* – *Director of Onboarding, Southwest Airlines*

"..the biggest reason why people fail or underperform has to do with the culture and politics of the organization…so I focus a lot on basically three things: how we are going to help this person adapt to the new culture; how are we going to connect them to the right people and help them form the right relationships; and how are we going to be sure that we really align expectations in every direction so that they're set up for success…"

-Michael Watkins – Author, "The First 90 Days"

Key #3 - Engage with One-on-One's

Consistency, clarity and focus. Set the meeting a regular cadence and stick to it like glue. That way as things come up that frustrate or perplex them, they say to themselves in the moment "well we're going to chat on Tuesday, and we can talk about it then". Be clear in advance about how you'll spend time. It could be "Next week I want to talk KPI's" or "hey let's talk turnover on Monday". Doing that in advance helps them feel prepared and trusted. You want them to look forward to these, not dread them as "gotcha" sessions. Then it's simple.......focus. Shut off the phone, ignore the I-watch. Focus more on asking open ended questions than making statements. Get them talking, then listen intently. If you can actively listen, you get what you asked for and so much more. Your team needs to know that at that moment there is nothing more important than them, doesn't matter if it's 15 minutes or an hour. If you take that time now in a structured environment, it will actually save you a dozen messy interactions and phone calls in the field. The more direct reports you have, the more important this becomes.

-Pat Peterson - Senior VP of Restaurants, Wagamama USA, NY

An effective 1 on 1 only happens when there is two-way dialogue. Key steps I use in the process are simple but at times can be overlooked. I like to refer to it as P4. Purpose, Preparation, Presentation & Path. People's beliefs are driven by their experiences so remembering to follow through on all these steps improve the probability of desired impact. Purpose, one must have a clear understanding of the desired outcome before engaging in a 1 on 1. Preparation is developed based on that Purpose and Presentation me coincide with one's desired outcome. Path is the roadmap to achieve your Purpose and it is uber important at this point you validate clarity and commitment to the receiving party. This format can be used effectively in more than traditional 1 on 1's and I have found affective in accomplishing commitment and desired results.

-Paul Baldasaro – COO, Taco Mac, Atlanta GA

During a 1-on-1, I allow my employees to lead the conversation. This time is for them, not me. I listen, answer questions, and gain insight on their goals and needs.

-Julie Thompson – Senior Instructional Design, Zaxby's Grill, Atlanta GA

We break it down, in a People, Execution (operations), and Results process where it is the Manager's meeting and the supervisor is the listener. And the key as the leader is to ask one more question to help support the manager in their development.

-Gerald Pulsinelli – CEO, Viva Chicken, Charlotte NC

You can create a CADENCE OF ACCOUNTABILITY with your GMs by having a recurring 1-on-1 with them. The MOST IMPORTANT rule is to never cancel. This is a meeting that happens at the same time every week/month/quarter no matter what. Death, taxes and keeping the 1-on-1 meeting. The GM has a PRIMER that is a one-page document that has all of the most important metrics of the store on it. He/she fills out this PRIMER before the meeting. They do most of the talking. Let them lead by reporting out to you on their store metrics (mentioned above). In addition, the PRIMER has questions that prompts the GM to recite the yearly goals for that year and if they are on-track or off-track. There is another question that prompts the GM to discuss any challenges they are facing outside of their control? (ex: is there road construction happening outside of their store next week?) This meeting needs to happen at a non-peak time, on a non-peak day, to minimize distractions (ex: Every first Tuesday of the month at 3pm). After the meeting, ask them to give you a tour of their store.

-Steve Taylor – *Managing Member, CapQueen3 LLC, Charlotte NC*

Key #4 - Delegate By Creating Mini GM's

Delegating is one of the most important elements of leadership that is often overlooked. In most cases, people want to be given the opportunity to succeed and delegation allows that. I have found that by focusing on the individual project and how to delegate with it instead of a holistic person and their workload, you can be much more effective of a leader. Some projects, delegation has to be direct, while others you can be looser with based on the experience of the team being delegated to. (i.e The One Minute Manager)

-Alan Magee – *VP Marketing & Communications, Empire Portfolio Group, NY NY*

The art of delegating successfully is something that most learn over time. I like to break it down to a few simple checkpoints. Aptitude, Time & Desire. The individual you are working with must portray the aptitude, talent or even reach potential to successfully fulfill the task at hand otherwise it is doomed to fail right from the start. Secondly and probably the most important step is to evaluate if this person has the time to execute the task. To many times we don't look at this piece when delegating and wonder why potentially our "go to" team member failed at meeting our expectations. Finally, is desire. Choosing projects or tasks that interest that team member helps leverage the probability of getting the desired outcome. Take the extra time it takes to walk through these steps and there is less chance of having to return to repair the outcome.

-Paul Baldasaro – COO, Taco Mac, Atlanta GA

Delegation is absolutely essential the further you progress within an organization. This allows much more work to be completed, but equally as important, it allows people to develop their skills and the organization to have a greater level of buy-in on decisions and initiatives.

-Paul Macaluso – President & CEO, Another Broken Egg, Orlando FL

Key #5 – Leading with The Right Mindset

Managing is pure transaction, moving pieces from one place to another. It's very time consuming because generally the pieces don't move unless you're there to move them, or they move to places you don't want them to go.

Leading is about creating the image that you are someone people should want to follow. It's crafting the perception of how people see you. It's easily (and often) faked, but if you, your company, or your idea is not really worth following the trust you're given doesn't last long. It turns into animosity because people feel "fooled", that can quickly lead to a toxic culture. Conversely if you live the values you speak of, they will follow you anywhere.

Coaching is about crafting the perception of how people see themselves. It's starts with convincing them they should do a certain thing, then that they can do that thing, then showing them how and letting them fail safely until they can nail it, time and again.

Pick 2 of the above - I've rarely met someone who was truly proficient in all 3. As soon as I do, I'll be following them.

-Pat Peterson - Senior VP of Restaurants, Wagamama USA, NY NY

Managing – ensuring the vision is executed. Leading – ensuring the vision is communicated. Coaching – ensuring the team received constant feedback on performance.

   *-**Kimberly Grant** – Fortune 100 Director, Performance Food Group, Washington DC*

   In my opinion they are all closely related. Managing is executing a process, SOP, recipe, guideline that's been established by the company. A manager isn't always focusing on managing people but the process. Managing labor, food cost, beverage cost, plate cost, etc...

Leading is not only leading by example but leading through situational experience. Teaching and helping people to grow in their positions and understand what it takes to get to the next level. "I've been in that situation before and this is how I handled it".

Coaching is more directed towards personal development. "Can I give you some advice on how I would've handled that situation differently than you did"? "I was listening to the way you were speaking to that team member and if it were me this is how I would've handled it". You can never those words, always speak in a calm and forgiving voice, never curse, never yell, etc... Then circle back and check in with them to make sure you were understood and can you clarify anything else after it's processed.

   *-**Mike Moore** – Hospitality Executive, NY NY*

   In simplest terms, managing = Doing; Leading = Inspiring; and Coaching = Helping. To be a highly effective leader or team member, I think you have to be skilled at and willing to do all 3 at different times. Knowing when each is required and how best to do it is the art.

   *-**Coley O'Brien** – Chief People Officer, The Wendy's Company, Dublin OH**Key**

#6 - Master Your Meetings

Generally, I set the stage at the beginning of the meeting. I establish the needs/wants of the meeting and what I consider very important – the why. Without understanding the "why" we are meeting the dialogue often gets distracted and off course. "Why" gives a purpose to the meeting and feels less like a dissertation and more of a joint purpose.

-**Sean Keyes** – *VP Design & Construction, Focus Brands, Lancaster PA*

Always go into a meeting with a desired outcome, whether it is setting the stage for a future decision, building a key relationship, gaining a deeper learning or getting to a specific decision/outcome. If you state the objective up front (even prior to the meeting), then the group will be a lot closer to meeting the objectives. Additionally, a quick recap at the end making sure that everyone has their marching orders on what they are responsible for next.

-**Alan Magee** – *VP Marketing & Communications, Empire Portfolio Group, NY NY*

First is time. Meetings should be scheduled in 15-minute increments (vs. auto default for 1 hour). Second is content. All meetings should have an agenda which is shared in advance. One person should be responsible for taking notes and distributing after meeting ends.

-**Kimberly Grant** – *Fortune 100 Director, Performance Food Group, Washington DC*

Place time frames on each of your topics for the meeting that everyone can see and stay on time as much as possible. Don't be afraid to table topics that are not necessarily critical at that point in time in order to keep the meeting moving. Demand that everyone attending the meeting be fully prepared to present any relative topics within their departments in the same mindset. Gather feedback from each of your departments prior to the meeting so that they are part of the overall list of topics that is distributed prior to the meeting. Finally, no meeting should be longer than 45 minutes. After that you are losing your teams focus and potentially have to many topics to fully digest in one meeting.

-Paul Baldasaro – *COO, Taco Mac, Atlanta GA*

First, I always start meeting with an agenda that includes an objective; why are we meeting and what are we trying to accomplish. Next, if the meeting is a staff meeting to include department updates, I kick the meeting off with "weekly wins", where everyone chimes in with accomplishments for the last week, progress on key initiatives and even personal wins. The purpose of the weekly wins is multi-faceted, including getting the meeting started on a positive note, getting everyone to contribute, sharing appreciation for each other and general positivity. All these things help to build relationships and lead to collaboration on challenges that may arise in the remainder of the meeting. Finally, after the meeting, I think it's critical to send a recap with key decisions made and follow up items, including key owners and timing.

-Paul Macaluso – *President & CEO, Another Broken Egg, Orlando FL*

When I think about the best meetings, I've been a part of, I walk away feeling like progress has clearly been made, collaboration and alignment has been achieved, time has been well spent and resources have been well utilized. I've felt equally that way about 8-hour meetings and 15-minute meetings. Mastering meeting facilitation is both art and science, but at a minimum I think it requires having a clear and meaningful purpose, having a clear agenda, ensuring the right people are involved and engaged, ensuring all voices are heard and being respectful of people's time.

> **-Coley O'Brien** – *Chief People Officer, The Wendy's Company, Dublin OH*

Key #7 – Never. Stop. Training.

The staff that touches the guests are by far our most treasured asset. To be effective and successful, they must be challenged and constantly learning. They get bored so easily. The secret is to have a continuous program/workshop/time for learning set up on a cadence calendar. We conduct tastings of new items, tastings of core items, wine workshops that are hands on and have a story to tell, a new service technique, a new cocktail, etc....

If you're worried about your labor, make it voluntary and you'll see who truly cares. Those are the people you want to invest in.

> **-Mike Moore** – *Hospitality Executive, NY NY*

Implementing and maintaining a culture of learning requires consistency and motivation to meeting your long terms goals. Often times, managers lose focus on coaching and training their teams because they are busy with tasks. Overcoming this takes a constant drive to look forward at what the team could become.

> **-Julie Thompson** – *Senior Instructional Design, Zaxby's Grill, Atlanta GA*

Anyone who stops learning is old, whether at twenty or eighty. Anyone who keeps learning stays young.

-Henry Ford – *Founder, Ford Motor Company, Detroit MI*

Training is everything. The peach was once a bitter almond; cauliflower is nothing but cabbage with a college education.

-Mark Twain – *Writer/Entrepreneur, Redding, CT*

I fear not the man who has practiced 10,000 kicks once, but I fear the man who has practiced one kick 10,000 times.

-Bruce Lee – *Martial Arts Master/Actor, Kowloon Tong Hong Kong*

Right now, your competition is training.

-Unknown

Key #8 - The Art of Giving Feedback

Always be positive. People that love what they do generally are meaning to do the right thing. If there's an issue it most often was a mistake. Mistakes happen and being positive during the conversation, I believe, leads to positive change of behavior. With the right team everyone should be aligned in a common goal, so feedback (positive or negative) should be received well.

-Sean Keyes – VP Design & Construction, Focus Brands, Lancaster PA

I am very open, honest and forthcoming. If someone is struggling with another colleague or subordinate, I bring everyone together and get it all out on the table as difficult as it may be for everyone. Most people struggle with speaking openly and honestly in front of each other but it's the only method that truly works. If they won't speak up I'll say "Michael you're struggling with the way Ken is speaking down to you and I've heard him speak condescending to you, isn't that true? How does that make you feel"? That will start the conversation rolling and then you just play mediator.

-Mike Moore – *Hospitality Executive, NY NY*

When I provide feedback, I focus on how this information is going to help the receiver. Asking questions is a great way to lead someone to a conclusion they may not have come to without guidance and support.

-Julie Thompson – *Senior Instructional Design, Zaxby's Grill, Atlanta GA*

Always begin with giving them a "Charitable assumption" as we don't know what they may be going through at that time and to listen with the intent to understand.

-Gerald Pulsinelli – *CEO, Viva Chicken, Charlotte NC*

The reciprocation of feedback varies from person to person, this is why I try to always provide a bit of positive with the not so positive and bring solutions for improvement along with how the feedback is linked to our company mission and employee development. I've found sharing feedback in a timely manner is most effective along with tailoring the message with strategic facts rather than personal opinions. Finally, I make feedback conversational where both parties come up with solutions. This helps create ownership, investment and accountability.

-Ranita Bullock – *Corporate Catering Manager, Brock & Company, Inc.*

A technique I learned earlier in my career was referred to as SBI . . . Situation, Behavior and Impact. What is going on and what point do you need to get across (situation)? What behavior is needed (or needs changed) (Behavior)? What impact is desired or expected (Impact)? It's pretty simple, but as I prepare to communicate or coach a team member, I try and ensure my point of view and message is clear in those three areas.

   -*Coley O'Brien* – *Chief People Officer, The Wendy's Company, Dublin OH*

Feedback is the breakfast of champions.

   -*Ken Blanchard* – *Author, Business Consultant, Motivational Speaker*

What is the shortest word in the English language that contains the letters: abcdef? Answer: feedback. Don't forget that feedback is one of the essential elements of good communication.

   – *Anonymous*

Always LEAD WITH POSITIVE. Point out the Positive. Catch them doing something RIGHT! There are two ways to potty train a puppy. Do you follow the puppy around the house with a rolled-up newspaper and wait for him/her to use the bathroom on the carpet and then "pop" them on the bum with the rolled-up newspaper and say "no" or "bad dog"? This is a terrible experience for the puppy, and they learn to fear you quickly. In fact, maybe they don't want to be around you at all. Or is it better to proactively take the puppy outside every two hours and wait for them to use the bathroom and then CELEBRATE SUCCESS with the puppy? Great job! Way to go potty outside! Then give them a treat every time they use the bathroom outside. The puppy will catch on quickly. This is kind of a silly example, I know, but the puppy will respond way better to the positive reinforcement. The puppy wants to please people around him/her. When you walk into a store, or you kick off your meetings, always spend the first 15 minutes CELEBRATING SUCCESS. Maybe someone received a high score on a Food Safety Audit that week? Maybe someone received 3 five star reviews that week. Get in the practice of recording and logging great achievements within your group every day or week, and then CELEBRATE SUCCESS by reciting these achievements in front of their peers or their team. Leading with positivity and celebrating success will soon trickle down through your organization. You will soon find your GMs celebrating success with their subordinates, thus leading to a positive work culture.

-Steve Taylor – *Managing Member, CapQueen3 LLC, Charlotte NC*

Key #9 - Closing The Gap

Closing the gap between guest expectations and operator execution takes intentional training, planning, and empathy. You must not only put yourself in the position of the guest, but also be able to train and coach your team to do the same. It requires continual focus on your people so they stay motivated to focus on your guests.

-Julie Thompson – *Senior Instructional Design, Zaxby's Grill, Atlanta GA*

Always put ourselves in the seat of the guest, see thru their eyes and ask ourselves what would I would expect from our dining experience.

-Gerald Pulsinelli – *CEO, Viva Chicken, Charlotte NC*

Get closer than ever to your customers. So close that you tell them what they need well before they realize it themselves.

-Steve Jobs – Founder, Apple Inc., Palo Alto CA

If you're competitor-focused, you have to wait until there is a competitor doing something. Being customer-focused allows you to be more pioneering.

-Jeff Bezos – Founder, Amazon, Seattle WA

What gets measured gets managed! Customer Experience quantified is 90% or greater all the time. So, we generally would close the gap between customer perception vs. reality by tracking the internal metrics of each restaurant. What was the score of the last 3rd-party Food Safety Audit? What was the score of the last county food safety inspection?

1. What was the score of the last unannounced Franchisor inspections?

2. What is the average of the customer satisfaction scores over the last 3 months? (Nineties are NICE, eighties are unacceptable!)

3. How many 5 star google reviews have you had in the last 3 months?

4. Once we aggregate all of these scores, how does your stack rank compare against the rank of your peers in our system?

5. How does the stack rank of our system compare to that of the entire franchise?

We can close the gap by improving all of these scores individually first. You really start to get a good picture of how your operations are going by aggregating all of the metrics.

-Steve Taylor – Managing Member, CapQueen3 LLC, Charlotte NC

Key #10 - Using The Power of Influence

Influence is the greatest untapped power within any organization. It is a internally developed trait within an individual but it's derived from a simple premise- respect. The influencers in your organization regardless of title or position command the respect of people at multiple levels; so much so that people actually seek their counsel.

-*Pat Peterson* - *Senior VP of Restaurants, Wagamama USA, NY NY*

They achieve that respect through continued delivery of results, genuinely listening to others and most importantly they have a heart of service. They genuinely want to see others succeed and take their time to help make that happen. That investment over time earns the their "influencer" status. It can't be bestowed by leadership. You can't create them, but you can do two things to use it to your advantage;

1.) Create an environment where they can connect at all levels. I had the President of a company call me into her office unexpectedly once. She started by saying she has heard from many people how I had taken my time to help them through problems unrelated to my job, talk to them, listen and connect with them. I thought I was in trouble for being unproductive, but she said "what you're doing is some of the most valuable time you will spend for this organization, so no matter what else is going on if you feel like you need to spend time connecting and talking with someone, do it. Every time."

2.) Second, identify the true influencers and touch base to get their pulse, sell them on the goals before going out to the larger group. Be subtle, overt attempts will give them a big head and you'll lose them (or rather, they'll lose themselves). Identifying them takes time; and the one who tells you they have influence rarely does. You have to ask your team who they trust, whose counsel they seek or who they want to be like. Then follow the names that repeat. It's often someone you don't expect because their nature is to spend more time helping others than preening and talking about themselves.

-**Pat Peterson** - *Senior VP of Restaurants, Wagamama USA, NY NY*

Influencers are the quiet currents that can work for you or against you. They are the "exponential" factor in any initiative or mission.

-**Pat Peterson** - *Senior VP of Restaurants, Wagamama USA, NY NY*

Influence all comes down to relationships, no matter what level of the organization you may be. Influence is like tokens at an arcade, you collect them by strengthening your relationships with people over time and then when you need to redeem them for a prize or to play a game, you can easily.

-**Alan Magee** – *VP Digital Marketing & Technology, Church's Chicken, Atlanta GA*

The best lesson in influence is to put a person in a position of indirect vs. direct power. This can be achieved by creating work stream teams with a "lead" or can be created by dotted line relationships. Any opportunity to flex a consensual/influential style vs. command and control is great for the development of leaders in today's business.

-**Kimberly Grant** – *Fortune 100 Director, Performance Food Group, Washington DC*

I would ask them to reflect on a time that someone made them feel special. Once they had that in mind, I would ask them if they would perform at a higher level for that person. Then, I would ask them to think about the techniques that person used to make them feel special and to put together an action plan to put those things into practice.

*-**Paul Macaluso** – President & CEO, Another Broken Egg, Orlando FL*

People I've viewed as being skilled at the art of influencing demonstrated very similar attributes... they knew what they were talking about (knowledgeable); they knew how to communicate appropriately their audience (relatable); and people believed what they were saying (trustworthy). I'm not saying those are the only requirements to being good at influencing, but I'm certain you can't be successful at influencing without demonstrating those three attributes.

*-**Coley O'Brien** – Chief People Officer, The Wendy's Company, Dublin OH*

On a Side Note – Sit Down for All Your Conversations

The stage needs to ensure the importance. Again, go back to the "why" we are in need of the action and set timelines. I also believe the timelines need to be realistic. Setting an unreasonable timeframe can often lead to inaccurate work as a result of the rush to complete. I'd rather give a little extra time, so thoughtful thinking is done.

*-**Sean Keyes** – VP Design & Construction, Focus Brands, Lancaster PA*

My motto is; honest, direct, consistent, fair feedback but nice about it. This has always worked well and as much as they appreciate the honesty, it sometimes hurts. To get the complete result I make sure it's all documented and followed through on in the next one on one. This is very effective.

*-**Mike Moore** – Hospitality Executive, NY NY*

On a Side Note – Write Down and Follow Up on Everything

There (are) so many distractions in our lives. Many professional distractions and deadlines, but also personal distractions. It can be daunting to master the balance of the two. I've found that there isn't one thing that works to keep you organized. Some weeks, it is post-it notes and then the next week is simple notes in my notebook. I love to sketch, and being in the design and construction field, I'm able to often get my thoughts down by doodling quick thumbnails, which triggers my thinking when I refer back to the sketches.

*-**Sean Keyes** – VP Design & Construction, Focus Brands, Lancaster PA*

On a Side Note – Explain the Why Before You're Asked

No matter the generation, the Why is what motivates people. If you don't share the "Why" then they will develop what the "why" is for themselves and often it is far from the reality. I find that by starting with the "Big" picture and then narrowing down into the task it helps people understand how what they are doing contributes to the overall team and company goals. It is also, helpful to ask after explaining if they understand and it makes sense.

*-**Alan Magee** – VP Marketing & Communications, Empire Portfolio Group, NY NY*

ABOUT THE AUTHOR

Jason Brooks has over 30 years of experience in the restaurant industry in multiple leadership roles with 6 of the Top 100 restaurant brands today. Jason coaches restaurant executives in the art of not just goal setting, but goal getting. He also teaches restaurant managers how to transform their management style to improve their hospitality leadership so they never lead alone again.

His background from 20+ brands has given him the unique perspective of seeing the Mona Lisa painted 20+ ways with the ability to take the best points of each one and apply them to teams today. He is an expert in creating bite-sized chunks of audacious goals, conceptual ideation, and communicating with all levels of an organization to help create step change. When not on stage, you can find Jason sautéing, smoking, or grilling something in his backyard with his wife and family!